53 READY-TO-USE
KAWAII CRAFT PROJECTS

ALA Editions purchases fund advocacy, awareness, and accreditation programs for library professionals worldwide.

53

Ready-to-Use

KAWAII

Craft Projects

edited by **ELLYSSA KROSKI**

ALA
Editions
CHICAGO | 2020

ELLYSSA KROSKI is the director of information technology and market-ing at the New York Law Institute as well as an award-winning editor and author. She is a librarian, an adjunct faculty member at Drexel University and San Jose State University, and an international conference speaker. She was named the winner of the 2017 Library Hi Tech Award from the ALA/LITA for her long-term contributions in the area of library and information science technology and its application. She can be found at http://amazon.com/author/ellyssa.

ISBN: 978-0-8389-1924-8 (paper)

Library of Congress Cataloging-in-Publication Data

Names: Kroski, Ellyssa, editor.
Title: 53 ready-to-use kawaii craft projects / edited by Ellyssa Kroski.
Other titles: Fifty-three ready-to-use kawaii craft projects
Description: Chicago : ALA Editions, 2020. | Includes bibliographical references and index. | Summary: "Kawaii, born in Japan, is the culture of cuteness, and its influence is seen world-wide in clothing, accessories, games, and food. Kawaii projects at your library will get a new crowd using your 3-D printer and introduce anime and manga enthusiasts to crafting. In her new book, Kroski has gathered creative and crafty librarians to share their most popular Kawaii programs."—Provided by publisher.
Identifiers: LCCN 2019027008 | ISBN 9780838919248 (paperback)
Subjects: LCSH: Libraries—Activity programs—United States. | Handicraft. | Makerspaces in libraries.
Classification: LCC Z716.33 .A14 2019 | DDC 025.5—dc23
LC record available at https://lccn.loc.gov/2019027008

Book design by Alejandra Diaz in the Tisa Pro and Gotham typefaces.

♾ This paper meets the requirements of ANSI/NISO Z39.48–1992 (Permanence of Paper).

Printed in the United States of America
24 23 22 21 20   5 4 3 2 1

CONTENTS

Part III | QUILLING, ORIGAMI, AND PAPER PROJECTS 75

Part VI | VINYL CUTTING AND STICKER PROJECTS 171

Part VII | FOOD-THEMED PROJECTS 193

Part VIII | CRAFT PROJECTS 207

ACKNOWLEDGMENTS

I would like to sincerely thank all the knowledgeable experts who contributed programs to this book for generously donating their time to making this an outstanding resource for libraries.

PREFACE

Kawaii is the culture of cuteness in Japan. The kawaii aesthetic is evidenced in clothing (Lolita fashion), products (Sanrio's Hello Kitty, San-X's Rilakkuma, etc.), games (Pokémon's Pikachu), and even food (Hello Panda cookies) and has extended its reach across the globe.

53 Ready-to-Use Kawaii Craft Projects for Libraries is an all-in-one recipe book for kawaii, or "super cute," crafts and makerspace programming that is chock-full of practical project ideas for libraries. Projects range in cost, topic, and difficulty so there will be something for every size and type of library. Projects run the gamut from crochet, paper quilling, origami, and felties to polymer clay, jewelry, and 3-D printing and vinyl cutting projects. Each chapter includes step-by-step instructions, a materials and equipment list, as well as learning outcomes and suggestions for next projects.

Authors of these kawaii projects are knowledgeable professionals from the library field as well as crafting aficionados offering real-world programming ideas for public, school, and academic libraries. As more and more libraries incorporate maker-related programming, the need to plan engaging projects around these STEAM activities increases. This is a one-stop guidebook for how to do just that.

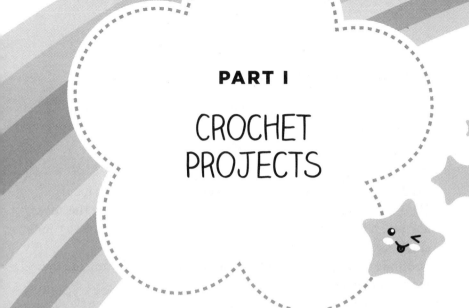

PART I

CROCHET PROJECTS

Introduction to Crochet

PENNY PAGE
Artist/Crafter/Woodworker

This is a beginner's introduction to American crochet with video tutorials and links to more information.

GENERAL CROCHET TERMS AND ABBREVIATIONS

- Contrasting color—CC
- Main color—MC
- Right side—RS
- Skip—SK
- Space—SP
- Together—Tog
- Wrong side—WS
- Yarn over (hook)—YO(h)
- Slip stitch—sl st

See more here: www.craftyarncouncil.com/standards/crochet-abbreviations.

BASIC AMERICAN CROCHET STITCHES

The two most common ways to begin your work are to chain stitch or magic loop (circle).

- **CHAIN** (ch)
    - Start with a slip knot.
    - Hold your yarn in your left hand however you can to keep it taut.
    - Slide your hook into the slip knot and wrap your yarn over the hook and pull it through. Slide it down to the middle of the hook so your stitches will all be the same size and won't be too tight.
    - Continue to wrap your yarn over your hook, and pull through for as many stitches as needed.
- **MAGIC LOOP** (ml; magic circle), used to get a tightly closed circle when beginning to work in the round
    - With the tail end of your yarn in front of your palm and fingers, loop the yarn around your index and middle finger to form an **X**.
    - Secure the working end of the yarn with your ring and pinky fingers.
    - Take your hook and insert it under the first strand of the **X** and over the second strand to bring the strand under the first strand of the **X**, twisting it while turning your palm to see the back of your hand.
    - Ch1 by grabbing the working end of the yarn. Take the circle off of your fingers. Unravel the end of the yarn and place it alongside the working end of the yarn to crochet it into your next step.
    - Crochet your first row into the circle. When your first round is done, pull the end of the yarn to close the circle. Sl st to top of first chain.
    Here's an excellent magic circle video tutorial by Crochet Guru: https: // bit.ly/2GzWuJy, or www.youtube.com/watch?v=gEq48ABHRZo.

BASIC STITCHES

SLIP STITCH (sl st)

- Insert hook through next stitch, yo and draw yarn through both the stitch and the loop on your hook.

SINGLE CROCHET (sc)

- Insert hook into next stitch, yo and draw yarn through stitch to the front. Yo again and draw yarn through two loops on hook.
- Here's a video tutorial from Lion Brand yarn: https://bit.ly/2SEcZeg or www.youtube.com/watch?v=EEP6njCSuTQ.

DOUBLE CROCHET (dc)

- Yo and insert hook through next stitch, yo again and draw yarn through stitch to the front (three loops on chain).
- Yo and draw yarn through two loops, yo again and draw through remaining two loops.
- Here's a video tutorial from Lion Brand yarn: https://bit.ly/2tcH4TR or www.youtube.com/watch?v=9Xq5nifQScI.

HALF DOUBLE CROCHET (hdc)

- Yo and insert hook through next stitch. Yo again and draw yarn through stitch to the front (three loops on chain).
- Yo again and draw yarn through all three loops.
- Here's a video tutorial from Lion Brand yarn: https://bit.ly/2Bts3kV or www.youtube.com/watch?v=WoiKayagPCo.

TREBLE CROCHET (trc)

- Yo twice, insert hook through next stitch.
- Yo again and draw yarn through stitch to the front (four loops on hook).
- Yo and draw yarn through two loops.
- Yo again and draw yarn through two loops.
- Yo again and draw yarn through last two loops. You will now have one loop on hook.
- Here's a video tutorial from Lion Brand yarn: https://bit.ly/2thIgFA or www.youtube.com/watch?v=GhmXX4yffa4.

Crocheted Puppy Nose Warmer

PENNY PAGE
Artist/Crafter/Woodworker

CROCHETED NOSE WARMERS have just recently become popular. They are being worn by folks of all ages and are so simple to make that even beginners will be successful. Participants will learn to read a pattern and use a crochet hook. They will also learn how to make four of the primary crochet stitches that can be used in many projects in the future.

The final step in making this cute puppy is cutting out and gluing felt pieces for the nose and ears. The eyes can also be felt, or they can be wobbly eyes.

Age Range	Type of Library Best Suited For	Cost Estimate
Tweens (ages 8–12) Young adults (ages 13–18) Adults	Public libraries Academic libraies School libraries	$15

OVERVIEW

- You can purchase one or two skeins of yarn and then make small balls for each participant. Each person will need their own crochet hook. Felt can be precut for ears and nose to save time.
- Use the slip knot to begin the project and not the magic circle, which is more difficult. It may not make a completely closed circle, but the felt nose will cover it.

- This is a wonderful opportunity to teach the art of
crochet. Participants will
carry this knowledge with
them for a lifetime. People
without prior crochet experience may need more
attention to begin with,
especially with the basic
way to hold yarn and cro-
chet hook. The good news
is that after the chain and
circle are made, there are
only four rows to this small
project. The ear loops are
just a repeat of the original
chain.

Figure 1.1 | Kawaii puppy nose warmers

- It is recommended that staff
make the ear warmer themselves to make sure they understand the
pattern. This will also determine how long the program will last. I make
mine in 15 minutes, but my guess is that it will take 45 minutes to an hour
for the session depending on previous knowledge of crochet.
- If the class is a mix of beginners and experienced crocheters, the staff
can be fewer than if the class is all beginners. All beginner classes will
place a staff member between two participants. So if the beginner class
is eight, the staff needed will be four.

Materials List

- One or two skeins of white 100 percent acrylic yarn (medium weight #4)
divided into small balls
- Crochet 5-millimeter (size I) hook for each participant
- Scissors, which can be shared, as they only will be used at the end of
the project
- Black felt
- Googly eyes
- White craft glue
- Toothpicks, or something to apply the glue to small pieces

- Copy of pattern for each participant (they may want to make more when they go home!)

Preparation

- Have a station where you can keep felt pieces, eyes, glue, and toothpicks.
- Have all pieces of felt cut into ears, nose, and eyes (if not using the googly eyes).
- Distribute yarn balls and crochet hooks. Decide whether or not you will send crochet hooks home with participants.
- Have participants sit at a table or in a circle in comfortable chairs or on the floor cross legged. The important thing here is to free them from stress so they will be receptive to instruction.

PROJECT INSTRUCTIONS

Introduction to Basic Crochet Stitches

Note: Detailed instructions on how to crochet these stitches can be found in the Introduction to Crochet section preceding this chapter.

- Explain how to read the pattern and abbreviations.
- Provide hands-on help for each participant on how to hold the crochet hook while keeping the yarn taut.
- Read one step at a time before executing it.

Stitches Used

- Chain (ch)
- Slip stitch (sl st)
- Double crochet (dc)
- Half double crochet (hdc)

To Start

- Use a 5-millimeter (size I) crochet hook.
- Ch4 and join with sl st to make the ring. Or use magic loop (ml).
- Ch3, 11 dc into ring (for child's size: ch9). Join with sl st to top of ch3.
- Ch3, dc in each st around. Join with sl st to top of ch3.
- Ch2, hdc into next st, * 2 hdc into next st, 1 hdc into next st *. Repeat from * around, join with sl st to top of ch2.

Figure 1.2 | The completed puppy nose warmer

Ear Loops

- Sl st into first two stitches.
- Ch45 (for child's size: ch40).
- Sl st into same stitch as starting point for chain.
- Sl st around halfway. Fold nose warmer to see where to place the second ear loop.
- Ch45 (for child's size: ch40).
- Sl st into same stitch as starting point for chain. Sl st around to first ear loop.

LEARNING OUTCOMES

Participants will . . .
- Organize materials.
- Read a crochet pattern and know abbreviations for needed stitches in this project.
- Use a crochet hook and execute four basic crochet stitches.
- Create a kawaii puppy by applying cut-out felt pieces and googly eyes to their finished piece.

RECOMMENDED NEXT PROJECTS

- Notice that the ear loops look like cat whiskers. This project can be offered again with any color yarn to create a cat, panda, or anyone's favorite character. It also can be made plain.
- The stitches in this project are a good knowledge base and, with additional stitches learned, can be used to make other crochet projects included in this book.

Cupcake Cowl

LILLIANNA KIEL

Creative Writing/Digital Humanities Undergraduate Student, Penfield Library

THIS CUTE CUPCAKE cowl will encourage beginner makers and crocheters—and even more advanced crocheters—to switch yarn colors within a project and allow experimentation with colors. It will also teach them how to work a project flat that will finish in the round and, of course, the bobble stitch! This simple cowl will experiment with different techniques and stitches that will build confidence in any crocheter to try mixing fun colors and stitches to create a warm, cozy cowl for the chilly months.

Age Range
Young adults (ages 13–18)
Adults

Type of Library Best Suited For
Public libraries
Academic libraries
School libraries

Cost Estimate

- $10–$25
- Yarns range in price depending on the yarn's content. Acrylic yarn will be more inexpensive than yarn made with materials such as wool and alpaca.

Figure 2.1 | Kawaii cupcake cowl

OVERVIEW

This project will entail having participants create a small scarf that will be sewed together to create a cowl. The program, if done in one increment, would take approximately two hours. If done in segments, the program could be broken up into two programs, each an hour long, or into three programs that could be 30 to 45 minutes. The program should be more than 30 minutes to give each participant a chance to ask questions. This project teaches multiple things so there will definitely be questions. There should be at least a minimum of three to four staff members, preferably staff members who have crochet experience. The groups should be capped at seven to eight people.

Materials List

- Three skeins of Worsted Weight yarn (370 yards/198 grams) each (the three yarns should resemble the cake of the cupcake, the icing, and the sprinkles)

Optional Materials
- For the original project, three skeins of Red Heart with Love were used. This yarn is soft and inexpensive, which makes for a great finished cowl. The colors used were taupe, bubble gum, and Aran.

Necessary Equipment

- 5.5-millimeter (size I9) crochet hook
- Darning/yarn needle
- Scissors

STEP-BY-STEP INSTRUCTIONS

Preparation

- Make sure to be familiar with single crochet, double crochet, and chain stitches.
- Practice the bobble stitch, if necessary: Yarn over, insert hook into stitch, and pull up a loop. Yarn over and pull through two loops on hook. Yarn over again, insert hook into same stitch/space four times and/or until there is a total of five loops on hook. Then yarn over and pull through all five at once.
- Make sure to be familiar with the whip stitch when sewing the scarf into a cowl.
- Make sure each color of yarn is a different color so the cupcake can appear in the cowl.
- Change yarn colors at the end of each row by looping the new color into current color loop, leaving a longer tail to weave in when finished.
- **Abbreviations:** dc (double crochet), sc (single crochet), ch (chain), bo (bobble stitch)

PROJECT INSTRUCTIONS

- **Row 1:** Chain 66.
- **Row 2:** Dc into third ch from hook and continue to dc into each ch remaining. Ch2, turn work (the ch2 *does not* count as a stitch).
- **Row 3:** Dc into each stitch across. There should now be 65 dcs. Ch2 and turn work.
- **Row 4–7:** Dc in each stitch across, ch2 at the end of each row and turn work.
- **Row 8:** Change the color of yarn to the color being used to resemble the icing. Ch2 and turn work. Dc in same stitch as joining and each stitch across. Ch2 and turn work.
- **Row 9:** Dc in each stitch across. Ch2 and turn work.

- **Row 10:** Change the color of yarn to the color being used to resemble the sprinkles. Ch3, turn work. Dc into the first stitch. * Bo in the next stitch, sc in the next. * Repeat stitches within the * until the end. The last stitch will be a sc.
- **Row 11:** Change back to yarn for icing color. Ch2, dc in the top of each bo and sc. Ch2 and turn work.

Figure 2.2 | Cupcake stitches closeup

- **Row 12:** Dc in each stitch across. After this row is complete, change back to sprinkle color.
- **Row 13:** Repeat row 10.
- Fasten off by chaining one and pulling down tightly to keep the project from unraveling.
- Place each end of the scarf together, and whip stitch them together using the darning/yarn needle.
- Weave in ends.

LEARNING OUTCOMES

Participants will . . .
- Learn to switch yarn colors within a project, promoting experimenting with different colors.
- Learn the bobble stitch.
- Learn to work a flat project, turning it into a project "in the round."

RECOMMENDED NEXT PROJECTS

- Chapter 1: Crocheted Puppy Nose Warmer
- Chapter 3: Heart Stitch Cowl
- Chapter 4: Sushi Roll Scarf
- Chapter 5: Dinosaurs for Small Hands

Heart Stitch Cowl

LILLIANNA KIEL
*Creative Writing/Digital Humanities Undergraduate Student,
Penfield Library*

THIS HEART STITCH cowl is warm, cozy, and full of love! The cute and easy heart stitch pops with any color and looks adorable on everyone. This cowl can also be modified—instead of keeping it short, it can be made longer into a scarf. It will provide makers and crocheters with a new stitch that can be used not only in this cowl but on any project and will allow crocheters to become more confident when approaching different stitches that seem complex but are super simple.

Age Range	Type of Library Best Suited For
Young adults (ages 13–18) Adults	Public libraries Academic libraries School libraries

Cost Estimate

- $10–$25
- Yarns range in price depending on the yarn's content. Acrylic yarn will be more inexpensive than yarn made with materials such as wool and alpaca.

Figure 3.1 | Final kawaii heart stitch cowl

OVERVIEW

This project will entail teaching makers/crocheters the heart stitch, and it's made for beginners to advanced crocheters. The program should take about two hours; there are quite a few different rows and techniques to be taught. Workshops or programs should be limited to a maximum of five to six people because it can be a little more difficult for beginners to learn. A minimum of two to three staff members should be present; a more intimate, one-on-one experience will benefit this project because it's, as stated before, more complex.

Materials List

- Two different colored skeins of Worsted Weight yarn (370 yards / 198 grams) each

Optional Materials
- Red Heart with Love in the colors hot pink and minty was used in the project example. This yarn is inexpensive and soft and makes for a perfect cowl.

Necessary Equipment
- 5.5-millimeter (size I9) crochet hook
- Scissors
- Darning/yarn needle

STEP-BY-STEP INSTRUCTIONS

Preparation

- Be familiar with a dc cluster.
  - **Dc cluster:** Yarn over, insert hook in stitch, pull up a loop, yarn over, pull back through first two loops on hook, yarn over, insert hook into the same stitch, pull up a loop, yarn over, pull through first two loops, yarn over, insert hook in same stitch again, pull through first two loops, yarn over, and pull through all loops.
- Be familiar with double crochet, single crochet, half-double crochet, and chains.
- Change yarn colors at the end of each row by looping new color into current color loop, leaving a longer tail to weave in when finished.
- **Abbreviations:** dc (double crochet), sc (single crochet), hdc (half-double crochet), ch (chain)

PROJECT INSTRUCTIONS

- **Row 1:** Chain 69 in main color. Dc in fourth chain from hook. (To make longer, or into a scarf, chain any multiple of 6 + 3 extra chains.)
- **Row 2:** Dc in each stitch across. Ch1 and turn work.
- **Row 3:** Sc in first stitch and each stitch across. The last sc should be in the top of the ch3 from previous row. That Ch3 counted as the first dc.
- **Row 4:** Change yarn color to the color of the hearts. Ch2 (this counts as the first dc of the dc cluster) and turn work. Work a dc cluster. Ch2, skip five stitches, insert hook into the sixth stitch and dc cluster, ch2, and dc cluster again all in the same stitch. This will form the heart. Repeat this to the end of the row, and the last heart will be a half of a heart. It will form one whole heart when the ends are sewn together at the end.
- **Row 5:** Change yarn color back to main yarn color. Ch1 and turn work. Sc in the first stitch, ch1, * HDC in the second, third, and fourth skipped stitch from the row of scs that came before the row of hearts, all while working over the ch2s in between the hearts. Then ch2 and sc in the ch2 space between the dc clusters and ch2 again. Repeat from * until the last dc of the previous row. When reaching the last cluster—which is the half cluster that ends the row—after the last hdc, ch1, and sc into the top of the cluster stitch. Then ch2 and turn work.

- **Row 6:** Dc into the ch1 space from the previous row. Then * work dcs into the next three stitches, work dc into ch2 space, work 1 dc into the sc in between the heart cluster and then a dc into the ch2 space. Continue this pattern, from the *, until you reach the last cluster—the half cluster, or half heart—that ends the previous row. Once you reach that, dc into the ch1 space and then dc into the last stitch. Ch2 and turn work.
- Repeat rows three, four, five, and six until you have four rows of hearts.
- Fasten off and weave in ends with darning/yarn needle.
- Whip stitch ends together.

Figure 3.2 | Cowl with hearts

LEARNING OUTCOMES

Participants will . . .
- Learn the heart stitch.
- Learn to work a flat project into a project "in the round."
- Learn to use two different yarns in a project.

RECOMMENDED NEXT PROJECTS

- Chapter 1: Crocheted Puppy Nose Warmer
- Chapter 2: Cupcake Cowl
- Chapter 4: Sushi Roll Scarf

Sushi Roll Scarf

SARAH HOWISON

Children's Librarian, Public Library of Cincinnati and Hamilton County

WHAT COULD BE better than a handmade scarf? A handmade scarf that looks like sushi! This striped scarf is bold and eye-catching, and when you roll it up, it looks like a giant piece of salmon sushi. This project is great for crochet beginners because it only uses one basic stitch: single crochet. And it uses a *lot* of single crochet. By the time participants are finished, they'll have enough practice that single crochet will be second nature—which means they'll be ready to try new stitches next!

Age Range	Type of Library Best Suited For	Cost Estimate
Tweens (ages 8–12) Young adults (ages 13–18) Adults	Public libraries School libraries	$20–$50

OVERVIEW

For this craft, participants will create their own narrow scarf that, when rolled up, looks like a salmon sushi roll. Crochet beginners will learn basic crochet stitches, which are linked in the instructions. Staff and volunteers should be familiar with basic crochet in order to help beginners. One staff member per four or five participants should be enough. Because single crochet does take some time to complete, this project works best as a start-and-take, or as a project created as part of a weekly club. Once participants have learned the stitch, the scarf takes three to four hours of work.

Figure 4.1 | Sushi roll scarf, rolled up, buttoned, and good enough to eat!

Materials List

- Pink yarn, 50 yards per person
- White yarn, 75 yards per person
- Black yarn, 50 yards per person
- Black thread, one spool

A skein of yarn can cost $3, or it can cost $30. Worsted Weight acrylic yarn is suitable for this project. It tends to be very inexpensive and often comes in large skeins.

Optional Materials
- Stitch markers to mark the end of a row, one per person
- 10 to 20 yards of yarn in other colors, to represent different sushi ingredients

Necessary Equipment
- Crochet hooks in size G, H, or I (4.0 to 5.5 millimeters), one per person
- Tapestry needle with large eye, one per person
- Sewing needle with small eye, one per person
- Buttons, ½ inch or ¾ inch, one per person
- Scissors

Crochet hooks typically cost less than $2 apiece and can be purchased in sets. Be aware that a set of crochet hooks may include a wide range of sizes, some of which may be too small or too large for this project. You'll know a hook is too small if it's difficult to pull the yarn through the loops, or if you can't catch the yarn effectively with the hook. If the hook is too large, the project will seem extra "holey."

STEP-BY-STEP INSTRUCTIONS

Preparation

- Before the program begins, consider having a volunteer divide your skeins of yarn into smaller balls for individual participants.

PROJECT INSTRUCTIONS

- Distribute crochet hooks and yarn to participants.
- Begin by teaching basic crochet stitches to all participants. A video lesson is available here: https://archive.org/details/TutorialCrochetBasics.
    - Creating a foundation chain starts at 12:29.
    - Single crochet starts at 17:00.
- Have each participant create a chain of 12 stitches using pink yarn. Then turn the work over so that the hook is back at the "beginning" of the row.
- To start the first row, make one single crochet in the first chain from the hook, then single crochet across the chain for a total of 11 stitches. Chain one, and then turn the work over so that the next row can begin.
- Single crochet in the first stitch and then single crochet across. Chain one and turn. Repeat until scarf measures approximately 12 inches in length.
- Single crochet across and then attach white yarn in the last stitch of the row. Cut off pink yarn, leaving a 6-inch "tail" at the end of your last stitch. Using white yarn, chain one and then turn.
    - For a tutorial in changing colors, see this video: https://archive.org/details/TutorialChangingColors.
- Single crochet across, chain one, and turn. Repeat until white section measures approximately 24 inches in length.
- Single crochet across and then attach black yarn in the last stitch of the row. Cut off white yarn, leaving a 6-inch "tail" at the end of your last stitch. Using black yarn, chain one and then turn.
- Single crochet across, chain one, and turn. Repeat until black section measures approximately 12 inches in length, or enough to wrap once around the white section when rolled up, beginning with the pink end.

Figure 4.2 | Completed scarf, about 4 feet long

- Buttonhole row: single crochet in the first five stitches, chain 5, skip one stitch, single crochet in the last five stitches.
- Cut off black yarn, leaving a 6-inch "tail" at the end of your last stitch. Pull tail through the last stitch to keep the scarf from unraveling.
- Distribute tapestry needles. Participants will weave in the loose yarn ends by threading the yarn onto a tapestry needle and weaving it back and forth through the same-color stitches until it's hidden. Cut off any excess.
- Roll the scarf up, beginning with the pink end, so that the black yarn forms the nori wrap on the outside.
- Attaching the button: Find the place where the loop in the last row overlaps the layer below, and mark the spot by poking the tapestry needle in place.
  - Have each participant thread a small-eyed needle with 1 to 2 feet of thread or embroidery floss and knot the far end.
  - After selecting a button, participants will sew it in place so that it lines up with the buttonhole when the scarf is rolled.

TROUBLESHOOTING

- Is the scarf getting narrower or wider as participants crochet? Make sure that each row has the same number of stitches (11, according to the pattern). Slipping a stitch marker into the first stitch of a row can help remind participants where the last stitch of the *next* row should go. (If stitch markers are not available, a paperclip can be used instead.)
- Everyone makes mistakes. When a participant realizes that there's a problem, they can gently pull the yarn on the hook to undo the previous stitches, working back to the mistake.
  - Crafters sometimes call this "frogging" because you have to *rip-it, rip-it!*

OPTIONS

- What kind of sushi is your favorite? Consider adding stripes of different colors to the middle of the scarf to represent different ingredients of your favorite sushi roll!

LEARNING OUTCOMES

Participants will . . .
- Learn simple crochet skills, which can be built on for more complex projects.
- Walk away with a completed, useful project to show off their new skills.
- Develop patience and troubleshooting skills that will be applicable in their daily lives.

RECOMMENDED NEXT PROJECTS

- What other kinds of food have a great rolled-up shape? Could you make a cinnamon bun scarf? A burrito scarf?
- Once participants have mastered basic crochet, they can use what they've learned and move on to more complicated projects—like the Cupcake Cowl (chapter 2) and Heart Stitch Cowl (chapter 3) in this book!

Dinosaurs for Small Hands

EMILY MITCHELL
Coordinator of Library Technology, SUNY Oswego

CAROL MITCHELL
Retired Teacher, Quilter

GROWN-UPS ALWAYS WANT kids to put on mittens when it's cold outside, but many kids don't want to wear mittens. You know what kids do want to put on their hands though? Puppets! So why not decorate a pair of plain, boring mittens to turn them into awesome dinosaur puppets a kid will be excited to put on? This project walks you through the steps of knitting and crocheting a pair of mittens and then giving your mittens dinosaur spikes, a mouth, and googly eyes so that getting a kid dressed for outside can be fun instead of frustrating. It also includes some tips if you want to do a shorter version of this project using premade mittens.

Age Range	Type of Library Best Suited For
Adults	Public libraries

Cost Estimate

- $6 per pair of mittens
- This includes the cost for consumables only (yarn, googly eyes, etc.).

OVERVIEW

Like any knitting or crocheting project, this one will take a fair amount of time to complete. If you're having people knit/crochet their own mittens, don't expect to hold a one-off program and have people complete their projects during it! If you have a group of mostly experienced knitters and crocheters, you can set this up as two separate hour-and-a-half sessions: one session to get people started on knitting and crocheting their mittens and one session a week or so later where everyone gets together to work on decorating the mittens. This assumes that participants will finish making the plain mittens on their own in between sessions.

If most or all participants already know how to knit and crochet, you should only need one expert on hand to lead the event, and the group size could easily go up to a dozen participants. The less experience participants have, though, the more experts you're going to want to have on hand. Make sure you have participants sign up ahead of time and give you some sense of how comfortable they are with knitting and crocheting so that you can plan your staffing accordingly.

It's worth noting that the mitten pattern included here uses both knitting and crocheting in order to make a nice, thick mitten that works up very quickly but still has a stretchy cuff that will stay on a toddler's wrist. Any plain knit or crocheted mitten pattern could take the place of the mitten pattern included; the important part is that the yarn be roughly Worsted Weight so that the crocheted decorations are easy to attach. If participants don't want to combine knitting and crocheting, or if someone is looking for more sizes, I recommend these patterns:

- "Mrs. Murdock's Mittens" (crochet) available for free on Ravelry: www.ravelry.com/patterns/library/mrs-murdocks-mittens
- "Classic Mittens No. 615" (knit) available for free on Ravelry: www.ravelry.com/patterns/library/classic-mittens-no-615

If you want to do a much faster, one-off mitten-decorating program, consider having participants bring in a pair of store-bought mittens. Googly eyes will attach just as well on those as they do on homemade mittens, and you can substitute sewing on felt dinosaur spikes and mouths instead of creating those embellishments out of crocheting.

Figure 5.1
Completed dinosaur mittens, ready for chomping on some snow

Materials List

- 120 yards of Worsted Weight yarn in the main color you'd like your dinosaur mittens to be
- 15 yards of Worsted Weight yarn in red or pink to use for the mouth and the dinosaur spikes
- Two sew-on googly/wiggle eyes, 12 millimeters in diameter (or similar)
- Thread for sewing on the eyes

Optional Materials
- Worsted Weight yarn in a third color, if you don't want your dinosaur spikes to be the same color as the dinosaur's mouth

Necessary Equipment
- 4.50-millimeter double-pointed knitting needles
- 4.25-millimeter crochet hook
- Yarn needle
- Regular sewing needle
- Scissors
- Chalk

STEP-BY-STEP INSTRUCTIONS

Preparation

- Print mitten patterns for participants to follow.
- If you want to save time during the event, divide up the ball of red/pink yarn into roughly 15-yard pieces ahead of time. That way, you only have to buy one ball, but participants can still all use it simultaneously.

PROJECT INSTRUCTIONS

Make the Mittens—Knit Cuff

- Cast on 28 stitches on double-pointed knitting needles.
- Working in the round, knit 1 and perl 1 around.
- Continue in this pattern until you have 2 inches of cuff.
- Bind off.

Make the Mittens—Crocheted Hand (Fits Toddler)

- **Row 1:** Working into the knit cuff, single crochet (sc) 24 stitches around.
- **Rows 2–5:** Single crochet around—24 stitches.
- **Row 6:** Chain (ch) 4 and skip four stitches for thumb hole. Continue sc around.
- When you've crocheted about 4.5 inches from the cuff, start decreasing in this pattern: sc 1, decrease, sc 1, decrease, and so on.
- Keep doing that until the hole is very small—you should only be able to poke a single finger through it.
- Using a yarn needle, draw the yarn tail through the front loop of each stitch, and pull tight. Tie off, and bury your end.

Make the Mittens—Crocheted Thumb

- **Row 1:** Sc around the thumb hole opening (eight stitches).
- Continue sc around until you have 1.5 inches of thumb.
- Using a yarn needle, draw the yarn tail through the front loop of each stitch, and pull tight. Tie off and bury your end.

Decorate the Mittens—Mouth

- Switch to your red/pink yarn.
- Starting at the base of the thumb, on the top (so it will look like a mouth when someone is wearing the mitten), slip stitch along the length of the thumb and then back down it.
- Tie off and bury your ends.

Decorate the Mittens—Dinosaur Spikes

- Switch to red/pink yarn (or your third color).
- Fold the completed mitten so that the thumb is underneath the main body of the mitten, as if the mitten were a puppet and the thumb were the puppet's mouth.
- Using chalk, draw a straight line along the center of the mitten from the cuff to where you started decreasing, near the tip.
- Starting at the end of your line nearest the cuff, sc 24 stitches along that line, working into the back of the mitten. Ch1 and turn.
- Working into the line of sc you just made, slip stitch [ss] 1, half-double crochet [hdc] 1, double crochet 2, hdc 1, and ss 1 (4 times)—24 stitches. Ch1 and turn.
- Working into the row below, ss 1, sc 1, hdc 2, sc 1, ss 1 (4 times)—24 stitches.
- Tie off and bury your ends.

Decorate the Mittens—Googly Eyes

- Using a sewing needle and thread, attach the googly eyes to your mitten so that it looks like a cute dinosaur face.
- I recommend going overboard on attaching these sturdily, as they are likely to be tugged on, scraped against things, and so on.

LEARNING OUTCOMES

Participants will . . .
- Combine knitting and crocheting into a single project.
- Knit and crochet in the round.
- Gain experience turning plain accessories into something cute and fun.

RECOMMENDED NEXT PROJECTS

- Try designing your own cute mittens that look like something other than a dinosaur! Dogs, cats, bunnies, and so on are all possibilities.
- Try a project that uses some different knitting or crochet stitches, such as the Heart Stitch Cowl in chapter 3.

PART II

FELTIES, PLUSHIES, AND SEWING PROJECTS

Kawaii Coffee Cozy

SARAH HOWISON

Children's Librarian, The Public Library of Cincinnati and Hamilton County

CAUTION: THIS BEVERAGE is *extremely cute!* Participants will create their own coffee-cup cozy—or two or three. They make great gifts for any coffee, tea, or cocoa lover. The cozies are quick to make, and the decorations are only limited by participants' imaginations . . . and the contents of your craft-supply bin.

Age Range	Type of Library Best Suited For	Cost Estimate
Kids (ages 3–7) Tweens (ages 8–12) Young adults (ages 13–18) Adults	Public libraries School libraries	$10–$30

OVERVIEW

A coffee cozy is a quick and easy project that can be done in as little as half an hour. It's also endlessly repeatable, so participants who finish early can make a second cozy, as long as supplies are available.

Felt is the primary component of this craft. Embellishments of all types can be sewn or glued on, so feel free to empty out a bin of craft supplies and let participants loose!

Figure 6.1 | A Ghibli-inspired coffee cozy, using an altered template

A single librarian can run the program for 5–10 participants. For larger groups, a second staff member or an experienced volunteer is helpful.

Materials List

- Sheets or bolts of felt in assorted colors
- One empty coffee cup to help determine the size of the cozy
- Tacky glue

Optional Materials
- Thread or embroidery floss
- Tapestry needles
- Sequins, buttons, and so on

Necessary Equipment
- Scissors
- Sharpies (for tracing templates)

STEP-BY-STEP INSTRUCTIONS

Preparation

- Get coffee from your favorite coffee shop—and make sure to pick up a cardboard sleeve for the cup!
- If preparing the program for a very young group, consider cutting out some templates in advance to save time and frustration.

PROJECT INSTRUCTIONS

- Gently separate the glued ends of the cardboard coffee sleeve—this will be the template for the coffee cozy.
- Have participants select a felt color for their coffee cozy.
- Have participants trace the template onto a piece of felt.
- Distribute scissors for participants to cut out the felt shapes. Have them turn it over so that the marker side is facing down. That will be the inside

Figure 6.2 | A decorated coffee cozy

of the completed coffee cozy. (The project is right side up if the shape arcs *downward,* like a very small rainbow.)
- Let participants decorate the front side with felt scraps, buttons, sequins, or other items. Kawaii faces are especially recommended!
  - Centered designs look best when the cozy is finished.
- When all the items have been glued, have participants wrap the cozy around the empty coffee cup and place tacky glue on one of the overlapping ends. Hold in place for one to two minutes and then slide off the cup.
- To secure the ends while glue is drying, a stapler or small paperweight can be set on top of the overlapping ends. (But don't lay it over the *whole* cozy, or the glue may seep through onto the front.)

Options

- The template makes a flat-edged coffee cozy. Encourage participants to experiment with the shape. What could they create by adding animal ears to the top edge? Or paws to the bottom edge?
- Got thread and sewing needles? Consider including a brief sewing lesson and letting participants sew designs onto their project.

LEARNING OUTCOMES

Participants will . . .
- Create a cute, useful item that can be given as a gift.
- Learn to use and modify a template.
- Learn basic sewing skills with real-life applications.

RECOMMENDED NEXT PROJECTS

- Have participants figure out how to design a cozy for a mug. How might they work around the handle?
- Take your felt creations to new dimensions and create No-Sew Felties (chapter 12) or Cute Needle-Felted Critters (chapter 14), both projects from this book!

Binder Slime Squishy

MARISSA LIEBERMAN
Children's Librarian, East Orange Public Library

USING CLEAR BINDER sleeve protectors, tape, and slime, children can create their own unique squishy.

Age Range	Type of Library Best Suited For	Cost Estimate
Tweens (ages 8–12)	Public libraries	$5–$35

OVERVIEW

Clear binder sleeve protectors are the perfect material for creating see-through slime squishies. Children can start by creating slime from scratch at the library and then transition to the squishy activity. To make things even simpler, invite children to bring leftover slime from home and just decorate the squishy.

Materials List

- Sheet protectors or baseball card sleeves
- Tape
- Markers
- Clear glue
- Tide detergent
- Water
- Cups
- Spoons
- Scissors

Optional Materials
- Food coloring
- Orbeez
- Glitter

STEP-BY-STEP INSTRUCTIONS

Figure 7.1 | Smiley squishy

Preparation
- Place tablecloths on tables.
- Place a small bowl with glue on table for every person.
- Place a small cup of Tide on table for every person.
- Place a bowl of water with a spoon on every table.
- Place a sheet protector on table for every person.
- Put out markers for sharing.

PROJECT INSTRUCTIONS
- Start by making the slime. Feel free to use your favorite slime recipe.
- Slowly add Tide to bowl with glue and mix. Add more Tide as needed.
- Add a few drops of water, and mix.
- Add food coloring and glitter.
- Take slime out of bowl and knead with hands until desired consistency is reached.
- Adjust adding more glue and Tide as needed.
- Place slime on the side and begin making squishy.
- Cut sleeve protector to desired size and shape.
- Decorate using markers.
- Tape all edges except for top closed.
- Carefully scoop slime into the binder sleeve.
- Securely close top with tape.

LEARNING OUTCOMES
Participants will . . .
- Learn to use slime in a new and creative way.
- Learn elements of chemistry by creating slime.

RECOMMENDED NEXT PROJECTS
- Chapter 12: No-Sew Felties
- Chapter 18: Kawaii Paper Squishy

Cat Attacks Yarn, a Quilted Wall Hanging

CAROL MITCHELL
Retired Teacher, Quilter

EMILY MITCHELL
Coordinator of Library Technology, SUNY Oswego

ART QUILTS DON'T have to be intimidating, even for sewers/quilters who may not think of themselves as "artistic." This project guides participants through creating their own small art quilt, suitable for hanging on a wall. The art quilt this project focuses on has a cat attacking a ball of yarn, but if someone in your group wants to draw (or print out and trace) a dog or any other animal doing something cute, the project's steps are very easily adapted. Sewers or quilters who may consider themselves to be "only crafters" rather than "artists" will gain experience and familiarity with art quilting ideas and techniques from this project. This will help them develop the confidence to undertake more such projects in the future and perhaps even design their own.

Age Range	Type of Library Best Suited For	Cost Estimate
Adults	Public libraries	Approximately $17

OVERVIEW

As with most quilting projects, this project is not suitable for a one-off event. Participants in this project will work their way through measuring, cutting, fusing, quilting, embroidering, making a hanging sleeve, and binding their quilts—all of which adds up to a sizable time commitment. This project will work best if your participants are a group of experienced sewers/quilters and you plan on about three or four weekly meet-ups where everyone brings their wall-hanging-in-progress to work on. Two-hour sessions will allow everyone to have time to get set up and make reasonable progress, even if they spend some time helping other participants. Participants may also work on their wall hangings at home, in between meet-ups.

Figure 8.1 | Completed wall hanging

If you're doing this project with experienced sewers and quilters, you will probably be able to support just about any size group for this project with a single project leader to demonstrate techniques and point people in the right direction. Your biggest limitation in that case will likely be workspace: Where do you have room and power outlets for that many people to set up their sewing machines?

Opening the project up to participants less familiar with quilting would be possible with a small group (perhaps six participants) but would definitely require more time, a much more structured format, and several experts on hand to help teach participants all the steps that go into a project like this.

Materials List

- **Fabric:** two 20 × 20–inch squares for front and back, plus assorted scraps of fabric for cat, about 13 × 12 inches for body and 8 × 6 inches for head; 18 × 13 inches for rug; a ball of yarn about 6 inches square; tiny scraps for the cat's eyes; two 5-inch squares for hanging triangles.
- **Batting:** 22 × 22 inches
- **Fusible web:** ½ yard
- **Sewing supplies:** needles, thread, yarn or embroidery floss for embellishments, scissors, pins, rotary cutter, 6 × 24–inch quilting ruler, and pencils or markers

Necessary Equipment
- Sewing machine (it may be helpful to use a special needle for sewing machines that is designed to sew through fusible web)
- Iron and ironing board

STEP-BY-STEP INSTRUCTIONS

Preparation

- Collect the fabrics that you will need such as recycled wool fabric for the cat and the rug and used cottons for everything else.
- Gather the sewing supplies listed above.

PROJECT INSTRUCTIONS

Read all directions before beginning.

- Cut out two 20-inch squares—one for the front and one for the back of your wall hanging.
- Take the 18 × 13–inch piece of fabric that you have chosen for your rug and cut it in half diagonally so that the bottom leg of your triangle is 18 inches and the right side leg is 13 inches. Pin or baste to bottom right corner of front square. Attach to fabric using machine or hand blanket stitch.
- Print the pattern pieces for the cat's head, body, and ball of yarn. The file is located at https://goo.gl/1yn7KG. Be sure you print at full size. The easiest way to do this is to open the file in Adobe Acrobat. After you hit Print, you should have a Poster option under Page Sizing and Handling. Choose that option, and check the box to turn on cut marks.
- Cut out pattern pieces for the cat's head, body, and ball of yarn. Flip your pieces over to the wrong side and place on a piece of fusible web, paper side up, and trace. This will ensure that your cat is facing in the same direction as the picture. Cut out four 1-inch squares of fusible web to use for the cat's eyes and pupils.
- Roughly cut out pattern pieces ¼ inch larger than each shape. You will trim the shapes after you fuse them to the fabric. For more information about appliqué with fusible adhesive, see www.youtube.com/watch?v=9CjL2bamUR0.
- Following the manufacturer's instructions and using an iron heated to the recommended temperature, press your pattern piece of fusible web, paper side toward iron, onto wrong side of chosen fabrics; let cool. Don't over fuse. The extra heat will cause the glue to harden and make the fabric stiff.
- Cut out fabric shapes on the pattern lines.
- Peel off paper backing.
- Place fabric shape on front fabric. Following manufacturer's instructions, fuse shapes in place on background to complete your appliqué picture. Fuse

the cat's body, head, and yarn ball to your front fabric. Lastly, fuse the four 1-inch squares for the cat's eyes and pupils trimmed to the desired shape.

- Use machine or hand appliqué to outline your fabric shapes. We used machine blanket stitch to outline the rug, cat, and yarn ball. Then we used hand appliqué for the cat's eyes, whiskers, and face.
- Make your quilt "sandwich." Place your backing fabric right side down, then your batting, and lastly your top fabric with fused shapes right side up.
- Baste your layers together using your favorite method. We used pin basting.
- Add quilting as desired, using either machine or hand stitching. We added straight line quilting in the rug area, the wall paper, and yarn ball.
- Have fun with your quilt! This project provides some basic pattern pieces to make a simple quilt. Add any embellishments you want to personalize your appliqué. I added braided yarn for my yarn tail. You could add additional objects, buttons, beads, lace, or scraps of fabric to your picture to tell your own story.
- Trim your quilt to the desired size.
- Make a hanging sleeve on the back. We used a triangle method that we found here: "How to Hang a Quilt on a Wall | National Quilter's Circle," www .youtube.com/watch?v=Y6Ek93YsY5Q.
- Add your favorite kind of binding. For more information, see "The Ultimate Quilt Binding Tutorial" with Jenny Doan of Missouri Star, www .youtube.com/watch?v=0vCWpxBRs20.

LEARNING OUTCOMES

Participants will . . .
- Benefit from a collaborative environment in which to brainstorm ideas for personalizing their quilts and making them more meaningful.
- Gain confidence that they can create an art quilt.
- Create a hanging sleeve for their quilt.

RECOMMENDED NEXT PROJECTS

- Try making an art quilt based on a different image of your own design or selection.
- Try making something 3-D, like an ugly sweater plushie (chapter 10).

Stuffed Animal Taxidermy and Dissection

LINDSEY TOMSU

Teen/YA Librarian, Algonquin Area Public Library District

STUFFED ANIMAL TAXIDERMY or dissection is a great creepy cute project for tweens and teens. The programs can be offered together or separated into taxidermy- and dissection-based events. It works well as a Halloween-inspired event, a general summer event, or even with home-school students by incorporating elements of science into the program. These programs are also highly recommended for those trying to reach tween boys who will take delight in destroying and repurposing something cute!

Age Range	Type of Library Best Suited For	Cost Estimate
Tweens (ages 8–12) Young adults (ages 13–18)	Public libraries	Under $5 per participant

OVERVIEW

The idea for stuffed animal taxidermy and dissection came about when my teens planned an entire summer reading program around the concept of 10 weeks of spooky things. Having done similar programs before, such as zombie Barbies and Franken-toys, they were looking for something creepy cute that would appeal to all ages and genders. Stuffed animal taxidermy involves picking a "specimen" among a group of small stuffed animals and then determining how to "taxidermy" the animal and display it like a trophy, whereas stuffed animal dissection involves "dissecting" a small stuffed animal like one would a frog in science class. Librarians can offer this program as a simple creepy craft or add educational elements of taxidermy and dissection concepts to the discussion as teens decide how to deconstruct their "specimens."

Most of these tween and teen programs run to an hour and a half in length, but this program can be accomplished in just an hour. The activity does not require any special artistic skills besides the ability to cut and glue. Based on each library's meeting room space, librarians may have to limit how many participants can be accepted based on space or glue gun limitations (though usually not everyone is using a glue gun at the same time). I have run this program with varied attendance between 30 and 50 teens and just one librarian supervising (as most of the steps are self-explanatory and creativity-based).

Materials List

Most of the supplies can be used for both stuffed animal taxidermy and dissection. The basic crafting supplies listed below may already be on hand in the library's supply closets.

- Assortment of mini stuffed animals about 3 inches in length
  - Recommend the 50-pack assortments available at Oriental Trading Company (www.orientaltrading.com)
- Assortment of wooden plaques (circle, square, oval, French corner)
  - Recommend the Walnut Hollow Birch Value Plaques available at Dick Blick Art Materials (www.dickblick.com)
- One medium-size bag of polyester flufferfill to share
- Assortment of colored felt
- Minimum of four T-pins for each teen

Necessary Equipment
- Scissors
- Mini low-temp hot glue guns and glue sticks

STEP-BY-STEP INSTRUCTIONS

Preparation

- Although it may be tempting to ask tweens and teens to bring their own stuffed animals, it is best to purchase mini stuffed animals. The difficulty with teens providing their own animals is that they may arrive with specimens much too large for mounting to the plaques, or they may feel they are OK cutting into the stuffed animal only to regret it once it's too late to stop!
- For setup on the day of the event, staff should have one table set up with the stuffed animals, plaques, and felt and a second table set up as the glue gun station (or, if able to, a few glue guns per table for teens to share).
- At each individual seating space, place a pair of scissors, a minimum of four T-pins, and a small batch of flufferfill.

PROJECT INSTRUCTIONS

- As these programs are creativity-based, show off any examples to teens before they begin. Encourage them to be creative and not feel like their final product must look exactly like the examples.
- For both programs, teens should begin by choosing their animal. Be aware that some teens may want to do more than one, so be prepared to explain why that may not be an option. If the library will allow more than one project, I recommend having participants wait 30 minutes (allowing time for latecomers) before they can begin a second project. If planning on doing the programs separately, tell teens you need to save supplies—they will understand.
- Next, teens will need to choose their plaque. To make preparation easier, the library could purchase all the same style and then place a plaque at each seat or purchase a variety and let participants pick their style.
- At their seats, teens will need to determine how they will display their animals. For taxidermy, the common option is to remove the stuffed animal's head, give it some more stuffing, and then attach it to the plaque (with hot glue) like a hunting trophy. They could also decide to display their stuffed animal more like an actual taxidermied animal by cutting open a seam, stuffing it more to be stiff, and then gluing the animal in a standing or sitting position on the plaque.

Figure 9.1 | An informal dissection of a duck's limbs

- For a "proper" dissection, teens need to cut open their animal along their stomach and pull back their "skin" to expose their internal organs (often a bag of poly beads). Using the T-pins, the teens can pin the skin open to the plaques. Using felt, teens can create little internal organs for the animals (heart, lungs, intestines, etc.) and glue them in their proper space. For a more "informal" dissection, teens could separate body parts and adhere them to the plaque in an interesting manner.
- **Optional:** teens can write a specimen "label" on the plaque.
- **Tip:** use the flufferfill to add more stability to the animals before using the hot glue or T-pins to adhere them in position to the wooden plaques.

LEARNING OUTCOMES

Participants will . . .
- Learn how everyday objects can be repurposed into art.
- Be educated about taxidermy and dissection concepts and procedures in a creative way.
- Hone their creative skills by deciding how to display their animals.

RECOMMENDED NEXT PROJECTS

- Encourage teens to be as whimsical or as technical as they want. If doing the activities as part of a science-based program, provide them with a list of taxidermy concepts and images of dissection models for inspiration.
- The library could invite a taxidermist to attend the program who could bring tools or small samples to explain how taxidermy is done and why people do taxidermy, or invite a biologist/zoologist to explain the purpose of dissections and how they help scientists.

10

Ugly Sweater Plushies

LINDSEY TOMSU
Teen/YA Librarian, Algonquin Area Public Library District

WANT TO OFFER an ugly sweater decorating program but have a limited budget to buy sweaters for participants or have participants who will forget to bring their own sweater? Promote an ugly sweater plushies program instead!

Age Range	Type of Library Best Suited For	Cost Estimate
Tweens (ages 8–12) Young adults (ages 13–18)	Public libraries	Under $20 for a group of 30

OVERVIEW

Ugly sweater plushies came about during a regular ugly sweater program. It seems a given that if a library offers a program that requires teens to bring their own item of clothing, there will always be at least one who completely forgets! These adorable little plushies occurred when I had a few teens show up sans sweaters. What could we do? We had an assortment of felt and decided to make a shirt-shaped plushie and decorate it with the additional seasonal items meant for the real-life sweater decorating!

Most of these tween and teen programs run to an hour and a half in length, but this program can be accomplished in just an hour. No special skills are needed except the ability to use scissors and mini hot glue guns. The program is very creativity-based, so one staff member on hand would be enough to monitor the program. Program budgets will dictate how many supplies can be purchased, which, in turn, dictates how many participants can attend. For $20 in supplies, this program can accommodate an average of 30 teens.

Figure 10.1 | A simple festive ugly sweater plushie

Materials List

- Assortment of felt
    - Recommend felt by the yard available at Dick Blick Art Materials (www.dickblick.com)
- Assortment of easy-to-glue seasonal trimmings, which can all be shared among participants (check local Dollar Tree store). Examples include the following:
    - Tinsel and garland lengths
    - Mardi Gras party necklaces (to mimic lights)
    - Assorted bags of mini ornaments (snowmen, bows, gift boxes, etc.)
    - Assorted seasonal foam stickers/craft appliques (snowflakes, deer, trees)
    - Pom-poms
    - Googly eyes
    - Assorted ribbons
    - Clip-on fake birds (two-packs)
- One medium-size bag of polyester flufferfill to share

Necessary Equipment

- Scissors
- Mini low-temp hot glue guns and glue sticks
- Black Sharpies
- Pencils

STEP-BY-STEP INSTRUCTIONS

Preparation

- Before the event, cut the felt by the yard rolls down to size. Size will be determined on the estimated number of participants. If expecting fewer, cut 10 × 10–inch squares for larger plushies; if expecting more, cut 6 × 6–inch squares for small plushies. A rectangle of 10 × 8 inches is recommended for medium-size plushies (as seen in the photo).
- For setup on the day of the event, staff should have one table set up with the crafting materials and a second table set up as the glue gun station (or, if able to, a few glue guns per table for teens to share).
- At each individual seating space, place a pair of scissors, a pencil, and a few Sharpies to share.

PROJECT INSTRUCTIONS

- As this program is creativity-based, show any examples to teens before they begin. Encourage them to be creative and not feel like their final product must look exactly like the examples.
- Teens need to choose the color of their ugly sweater. Once determined, they will pick two pieces of felt. One piece will be the front, whereas the other will be the back of their plushie.
- Using a black Sharpie, draw a basic outline of a T-shirt on one piece of felt. Holding the two pieces together, teens should carefully cut out the shape.
- With the hot glue, teens will adhere the two pieces of felt together leaving the neck and top of the shoulders open for stuffing.
- Direct teens to choose what "ugly" components from the crafting/seasonal items they want to put on their sweater plushie. Once all materials are collected, they can experiment with the placement of the items.
- When teens have determined their design, they can begin hot gluing the pieces onto the felt. Some items may need more glue and time to dry depending on how heavy the item is.
- Once all the "ugly" components have been glued on, they can begin stuffing. Using a pencil, teens should start sticking bits of flufferfill into the plushie, starting with the bottom, up to the chest, and in the arms, ending with the neck area.
- When the plushie is adequately stuffed, teens can begin to hot glue the opening shut. They may want to alternate gluing a bit shut, adding more

fluff, gluing a bit shut, adding more fluff, and so on to make sure the top of their plushie is as fluffy as the bottom half of the plushie.
- Have teens look over the plushie and reinforce any decorations that may need some more glue after being stuffed.
- **Optional:** add a ribbon to the back of the plushie and the ugly sweater becomes an ornament!
- **Optional:** add a large safety pin to the back of the plushie, and have teens attach it to their shirt! They're now "wearing" an ugly sweater!

LEARNING OUTCOMES

Participants will . . .
- Continue to develop creativity and imagination through hands-on crafting activities.
- Develop critical thinking skills by using disparate materials to construct a new item.
- Participate in hands-on crafting as creators, which enables them to participate in fun, lifelong learning opportunities.

RECOMMENDED NEXT PROJECTS

- Teens will be exposed to basic no-sew crafting projects. Ask members of the teen advisory board or other teen volunteers if they would like to be in charge of running the program for younger children.
- Teens who are interested in sewing can try the craft again but choose a sewing option instead of hot glue.
- For advanced crafters, suggest they try making mini ugly sweater plushies with needle felting tools.
- For an added STEAM element, the library can provide LED circuit lights and cell batteries (available on Amazon in large lots of 50- or 100-count for about $10 and $20, respectively). Teens can poke some LED lights into the felt and attach them to a cell battery glued inside to mimic actual tree lights in their sweater. Unfortunately, this option means the battery will eventually die. Adventurous teens could try adhering the cell battery to the back of the plushie and aligning the lights in such a way that their ends poke out of a small hole in the back where they can be attached to a battery to be turned on and off at will.

11

Stuffed Animal Fashion Show

LINDSEY TOMSU

Teen/YA Librarian, Algonquin Area Public Library District

WHY SHOULD KIDS have all the fun? Let tweens and teens relive their childhood by offering a stuffed animal fashion show! Participants bring a beloved stuffed friend, use a variety of crafting supplies to make an outfit for them worthy of *Project Runway,* and then compete against each other on the catwalk!

Age Range	Type of Library Best Suited For
Tweens (ages 8–12) Young adults (ages 13–18)	Public libraries

Cost Estimate

- $20–$30 for 30 participants
- Check the library's crafting supplies first! Most of what is needed is crafting basics. The main cost will be prizes if the library chooses to offer them.

OVERVIEW

Members of my teen advisory board originally devised this program idea for our tweens! The basis for it is to just be silly and goofy—kind of a more

Figure 11.1 | Pig and polar bear are getting ready to catwalk their lovely outfits inspired by '80s aerobic fashion!

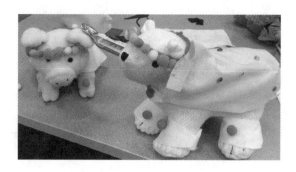

"mature" Teddy bear picnic program. Using basic crafting supplies, tweens and teens can make an outfit for a stuffed friend. The sillier the better! Those with a competitive streak can try to win prizes!

Most of these tween and teen programs run to an hour and a half in length. Give participants an hour to craft their outfit, and spend the last 30 minutes doing the catwalk presentation and awarding prizes. No special skills are needed except the ability to use scissors and mini hot glue guns. The program is very creativity-based, so one staff member on hand would be enough to monitor the crafting portion of the program, but an additional staff member during the catwalk portion is recommended to help take photos/video. Program budgets will dictate how many supplies can be purchased, which, in turn, dictates how many participants can attend. For $20 to $30 in newly purchased basic crafting supplies, this program can accommodate an average of 30 teens.

Materials List

- Teens should be asked to bring a stuffed friend from home! Larger sizes work best for this program. Worried teens will forget? If budget allows, grab a few back-up stuffed friends from a local Dollar Tree (www.dollar-tree.com), which usually has plush animals, plush dolls, and even some plush pet toys that would work.
- Assortment of felt
  - Recommend Felt by the Yard available at Dick Blick Art Materials (www.dickblick.com)
- Assortment of basic craft supplies (the more variety the better!)
  - Pipe cleaners, pom-poms, googly eyes, ribbons, foam stickers, beads, feathers, sequins, and so on
- Camera/phone to take photos of the event (especially the catwalk)

- Phone/music player to play a song during the catwalk (if doing the program with teens, I recommend "I'm Too Sexy" by Right Said Fred or "Supermodel" by RuPaul)

Optional Materials
- Tape measurers for teens to take measurements of their stuffed friends' heads, chests, waists, arms, legs, and so on
- I recommend prizes in the following categories: best outfit (as in looks like real clothing), most creative outfit, and best catwalk performance (all voted on by participants). I have used coupons to a local restaurant.

Necessary Equipment
- Scissors
- Mini low-temp hot glue guns and glue sticks

STEP-BY-STEP INSTRUCTIONS

Preparation

- Before the event, cut the felt by the yard rolls down to size. A rectangle of 10 × 8 inches is recommended, which gives a nice size sheet to work with for most projects.
- If awarding prizes, have some premade nomination sheets and pencils ready for participants to fill out during the voting process.
- For setup on the day of the event, staff should have one table set up with the crafting materials and a second table set up as the glue gun station (or, if able to, a few glue guns per table for teens to share).
- Set aside one table to be the "catwalk." Feel free to make it "fancy" (add a nice tablecloth, set up some LED tea light spotlights, place some chairs in front for audience seating, etc.).
- At each individual seating space, place a pair of scissors.

PROJECT INSTRUCTIONS

- At the beginning of the program, let teens know they will have an hour to create a fabulous outfit for their stuffed friend. Inform them of what time they need to be finished by so the fashion show can begin.

- As this program is creativity-based, show off any examples to teens before they begin. Encourage them to be creative and not feel like their final product must look exactly like the examples.
- Remind teens to be careful if they are gluing parts of their outfit around their "model"! No one wants to permanently glue a crazy outfit to their beloved stuffed friend!
- Teens will want to begin with a sheet or two of felt and will need to think of how complex they want their outfit. Just a shirt? Shoes? Hats? Knowing this, teens will use the felt as the equivalent of a fashion designer's muslin, which is used to make clothing patterns.
- After teens have their basic shapes made, they can begin adding embellishments to their designs with the basic craft supplies. Creativity is the key! Use felt scraps to make buttons, use pipe cleaners to create jewelry or shoelaces. The options are endless.
- Use the hot glue to adhere all patterns and embellishments together. Advise teens to remember to leave space for head, arm, and leg holes!
- Once the hour of design is complete, ask teens to take a seat in the audience. If there is a staff member taking photos/video of the event, make sure they are in place and ready to go. Start the music and, one by one, have teens help their stuffed friend sashay down the runway. If awarding prizes, remind them that there will be a prize for the best catwalk performance. (One of my teens, Austin, made a tiny top hat for his bear. When the bear made it to the end of the runway, Austin had a huge reveal as a tiny little creature popped out of the top hat! Needless to say, he won best catwalk for that surprise.)
- Once all models have walked the catwalk, ask teens to name their model and place all stuffed friends on the catwalk in a line. Pass out the prepared nomination sheets and pencils. Give teens about five minutes to vote. Tally up the results and hand out prizes!
- **Optional:** take one big group photo of all the designers and their models.

LEARNING OUTCOMES

Participants will . . .
- Learn that it is OK for them to just act like a kid sometimes and participate in a silly event.
- Have a chance to learn about fashion. (For a more educational angle, provide fashion books for inspiration [and possible checkout] or

actual sewing patterns to examine. A list could be handed out with definitions of basic fashion terminology. To make learning a bit more interactive, teens could be quizzed on fashion terms/history while they are crafting their outfit to test their current knowledge.)

- Build upon communication skills by working with their peers on projects in a collaborative and competitive environment.

Figure 11.2 | The hilarious promotional flyer for our stuffed animal fashion show

RECOMMENDED NEXT PROJECTS

- Taking inspiration from the most loved/most hated *Project Runway* challenge, hold the program again but task teens with creating an outfit out of unconventional materials (which could all be purchased for cheap at the Dollar Tree or ask patrons to donate supplies).
- For those teens looking to get more serious about fashion design consider offering a basic sewing skills program that will teach them the basic tools and knowledge to design something simple like a shirt, dress, or headpiece or go big and plan a multiday fashion workshop, which will cover basic terms, sketching, pattern making, and end with the creation of a simple design.
- For beginning fashion students, offer classic fashion-related programs such as tie-dye, deconstructed T-shirts, or jewelry making. For advanced fashion students, offer a fashion program similar to what many libraries have offered in the past, such as DIY duct tape prom dresses or a library fashion show showcasing teen designers.

No-Sew Felties

LINDSEY TOMSU

Teen/YA Librarian, Algonquin Area Public Library District

EVERYONE LOVES PLUSHIES! Tweens and teens can have a chance to make their own plushies of whatever they love!

Age Range	Type of Library Best Suited For
Tweens (ages 8–12) Young adults (ages 13–18)	Public libraries

Cost Estimate

- $20–$50 for a group of 50
- If you can splurge and stock up on felt or flufferfill, you will have leftovers for similar future programs.

OVERVIEW

No-sew plushies are a creative all-ages craft that will bring in both girls and boys. No real artistic talent is needed—just an idea of a plushie participants want to bring to life. The program can be run multiple times under different themes as well. Over the years, I have successfully offered it as no-sew emoji plushies, no-sew fast food plushies, no-sew monsters, no-sew felty freaks, and more. Of course, participants shouldn't be limited to the

theme of the program anyway—
let them create whatever they
desire (once I had a boy create a
carnivorous loaf of bread!).

Most of these tween and teen
programs run to an hour and a
half in length. For the No-Sew
Plushies, this is usually enough
time for the very detailed crafters
to make one plushie while giving
those who are quicker crafters
the chance to make two if given

Figure 12.1 | A lovely plushie plate of pasta

the option. No special skills are needed except the ability to use scissors and
mini hot glue guns. The program is very creativity-based so one staff member
on hand would be enough to monitor the program. As the supplies are basi-
cally just felt and flufferfill, the final cost will be determined by how large the
plushies will be and if the budget allows for stocking up on supplies at once for
future programs. For $20 to $50 in supplies, this program can accommodate
an average of 50 teens.

Materials List

- Assortment of felt
  - Recommend Felt by the Yard available at Dick Blick Art Materials
    (www.dickblick.com)
- One to three medium-size bags (or the 10-pound box option, available
  for around $20 at most Walmart stores with a crafting department, for
  cost savings and easier storage) of polyester flufferfill to share depending
  on plushie size
- Assortment of basic crafting supplies for details
  - Googly eyes
  - Pipe cleaners
  - Ribbons

Optional Materials

- Scratch paper and pencils for any teens who may want to sketch out their
  design before they begin cutting and gluing

Necessary Equipment

- Scissors
- Mini low-temp hot glue guns and glue sticks

STEP-BY-STEP INSTRUCTIONS

Preparation

- Before the event, cut the felt by the yard rolls down to size. Size will be determined by the estimated number of participants. If expecting fewer, cut 10 × 10–inch squares for larger plushies; if expecting more, cut 6 × 6–inch squares for small plushies. A rectangle of 10 × 8 inches is recommended for medium-size plushies (as seen in the photo).
- For setup on the day of the event, staff should have one table set up with the crafting materials and a second table set up as the glue gun station (or, if able to, a few glue guns per table for teens to share).
- At each individual seating space, place a pair of scissors.

PROJECT INSTRUCTIONS

- As this program is creativity-based, show off any examples to teens before they begin. Encourage them to be creative and not feel like their final product must look exactly like the examples.
- Once teens have their design in mind, they will need to pick their primary plushie color. They will need two sheets of felt—one for the front and one for the back.
- If the library offers a lot of felt crafting programs, consider starting a felt junk box of decent-size scraps. Remind teens to not take a full-size sheet of felt and cut out a small shape right in the middle! Instead, cut out smaller pieces from the outside edges in so remnants can be saved for someone else. Teens can use these smaller pieces for any details they will be adding to their design.
- After they have cut out the main shape of their plushie (whether a circle for an emoji or a body shape for a monster), they will need to begin the no-sew process. With the hot glue, adhere the two pieces of felt together leaving a decent space open for stuffing (top of the head, one side of the shape, etc.).

- Once all their decorative details are cut to size and ready to be applied, have teens experiment with the placement of the details and then adhere them with the hot glue.
- Once they are done gluing all their decorative pieces to their plushie, they can begin stuffing. Using a pencil, start sticking bits of flufferfill into the plushie starting with the bottom and finishing at the opening.
- When the plushie is adequately stuffed, teens can begin to hot glue the opening shut. They may want to alternate gluing a bit shut, adding more fluff, gluing a bit shut, adding more fluff, and so on to make sure the top of their plushie is as fluffy as the bottom half of the plushie.
- Look over the plushie and reinforce any decorations that may need some more glue after being stuffed.
- **Optional:** name your plushie and love it forever!

LEARNING OUTCOMES

Participants will . . .
- Continue to develop creativity and imagination through hands-on crafting activities.
- Develop critical thinking skills by using disparate materials to construct a new item.
- Participate in hands-on crafting as creators, which enables them to participate in fun lifelong learning opportunities.

RECOMMENDED NEXT PROJECTS

- This program can be repeated with an infinite number of themes! The first program could be a simple plushie design (like an emoji) and increase in complexity/creativity as the program is repeated.
- This program can be taken into advanced mode by offering teens the option to actually sew. Grab a few sets of sewing needles and thread, and have them available for teens who want to try sewing (maybe beginning with just sewing the plushie together and moving on to also sewing the details). Keep in mind this option may require an increase in program time.

Make Your Own Kawaii Popsicle Squishy

SARAH SIMPSON

Youth Services Librarian, Westerville Public Library

CAPTURE YOUR T(W)EENS attention with this sensory-stimulating and on-trend kawaii craft. Who doesn't love a squishy? Nothing relieves stress and inspires fun more than an adorable kawaii squishy. The materials for this craft are easy to come by and versatile, so if you don't use them up for this program, they can be used for other projects. And the level of difficulty can easily be adjusted to make a program that suits middle grades and up.

This project is as much about the process as the outcome and, of course, having a lot of fun from start to finish. Participants will start with a chunk of foam and some puffy paint and will end with a truly interactive piece of art. In the era of YouTube crafting, the DIY squishy holds a large market share, so should your attendees want to explore squishy crafting further, there are plenty of tutorials online.

Age Range	Type of Library Best Suited For
Tweens (ages 8–12) Young adults (ages 13–18) Adults	Public libraries School libraries

Cost Estimate

- $3.50 per person

- This is the cost of supplies that are most likely not readily available in your library's supply cabinet, such as the memory foam mattress topper, disposable gloves, and puffy paint.

Figure 13.1 | Kawaii Popsicle squishy

OVERVIEW

I created this kawaii Popsicle squishy program for teens, but if you want to presculpt the Popsicle shapes prior to the program, it is easily adaptable for tweens or middle grades. If you precut the Popsicle shapes, the focus of the program will be on painting and decorating. The painting will require some skill, but with clear directions and a great example, it should be easy.

Limiting attendance will make a better program for all. One adult to every six teens tends to be a good ratio so everyone is getting plenty of help when needed. Teens will likely have questions about sculpting their shape and need your guidance, so be prepared to offer it as they move through the steps. This program should be an hour in length to give participants plenty of time to sculpt and paint.

Materials List

- Flat nongel white memory foam with a 2-inch depth (the most cost-effective option is buying a 2-inch-deep memory foam mattress topper in twin or twin XL size, but memory foam is available in smaller, more expensive 10 × 10–inch squares for crafting as well)
- Pair of sharp scissors for each participant
- Popsicle sticks (each participant will need one, but they can splinter when cut, so have extras on hand)
- Two pairs of disposable gloves for each participant
- Light-colored washable markers for tracing
- 4-ounce bottle of black puffy paint
- Three 4-ounce bottles of white puffy paint (colors optional)
  - Buying white puffy paint in 4-ounce bottles and mixing in acrylic you have on hand is the cheapest option and will create great pastel

colors for teens' Popsicles. You can also buy solid colors in the 1-ounce multipacks or in 4-ounce multipacks. Each Popsicle will require about 2 ounces of puffy paint total.

- Popsicle template of choice (the template that I found online was 5 × 3 inches)
- Multicolored sprinkles
- Two 4-ounce bottles of liquid glue (white or clear)
- One roll of aluminum foil
- Toothpicks (several for each teen)
- Sharpened pencil for each teen
- Baby wipes

Optional Materials
- Small brush for detail painting; however, this can be achieved with a sharpened pencil
- Adhesive lint roller for easy foam cleanup

Some of these supplies will likely be on hand in your library (toothpicks, glue, aluminum foil, scissors, paper, markers, and Popsicle sticks), while others require special purchase. If you are a savvy online shopper, you can find a 20-inch memory foam mattress topper in twin size for around $27. I would recommend comparing the prices of the twin and twin XL mattress toppers because oftentimes the irregular size of the twin XL means that it is cheaper. Buying a mattress topper will provide enough memory foam for approximately 150 squishies, so you can repeat this program many times over.

STEP-BY-STEP INSTRUCTIONS

Preparation

The preparation for this program is minimal. You will need to cut the memory foam into rectangles that measure approximately ½ inch outside your chosen template so that teens will have extra memory foam to allow for sculpting mistakes. Each paper Popsicle template will need to be cut ahead of time. If you choose to do this program with middle grade kids, I would highly recommend presculpting the Popsicle shapes. Be prepared to demonstrate proper cutting techniques to achieve the rounded look. After the initial shape is cut out, sculpting should be a series of tiny cuts. It helps to watch YouTube demonstrations of this prior to the program.

PROJECT INSTRUCTIONS

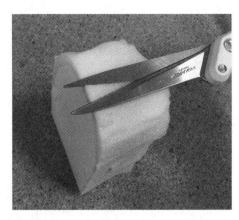

Figure 13.2 | Rounded top of popsicle squishy

- The Popsicle template should be traced on one side of each teen's chunk of foam using the light-colored washable marker. It is helpful to line up the template with the straight edges on the foam chunk so sculpting and cutting are minimized.
- The initial shape should be cut about a centimeter outside of the lines so that there is room for sculpting. Cutting through the foam will take some effort. Keep in mind that this is the rough form and more detailed cutting will be required to get it to have the rounded edges and top.
- The Popsicle should be sculpted to have a rounded top and slightly rounded edges and corners. This will involve turning the shape and making small cuts to achieve the desired shape (see figure 13.2). Sculpting should take anywhere from 15 to 25 minutes. Urge teens not to strive for perfection because those perfectly rounded squishies are produced by machines.
- Create the "bite" in the Popsicle by pinching the foam with your fingers. Pinch a semicircle of foam out in small pieces. By pinching, you are creating a more realistic-looking bite shape.
- Create an incision with scissors in the center of the bottom of the shape for your Popsicle stick. Cut the stick so that it is ¾ its original size. Insert the stick into the foam so that around 2 inches of it is sticking out. It may not go in easily the first time, and, if this is the case, have teens reinsert their scissors and widen and/or deepen the hole.
- Use the liquid glue on either side of the positioned Popsicle stick to affix it in place. No dry time is needed.
- Once teens are happy with their shape and their Popsicle stick is placed, it is time for paint. Each teen should create a small aluminum foil paint "palette" and mix 1 ounce of white puffy paint with the acrylic color of their choice with a toothpick until the desired shade is reached. (If solid

colors of puffy paint are used, then omit the mixing step because the paint can be applied directly to the foam.) Have each teen also tear off an additional piece of aluminum foil that they can rest their squishy on while painting the kawaii face.

- At this point, each participant should put on their first pair of disposable gloves. Scoop some of the paint off of the palette with fingers and rub it into the squishy surface (or apply directly from the bottle of solid color paint onto the squishy). Massaging the paint onto the surface is not only fun but creates a really uniform paint application.

- Once the squishy is covered in a uniform layer of paint, it is time to create the kawaii face. Set the squishy on the aluminum foil resting square. Squirt a small pool of black puffy paint onto the aluminum foil painting palette.

- Dip the eraser side of the pencil into the pool of paint and coat it with a generous layer of paint and dab it once about ⅓ the distance up the Popsicle shape. Repeat for the second eye.

- Dip the sharpened point of the pencil in the black puffy paint. (This can also be done with a small detail brush.) Create a "u" shape for the mouth centered between the eyes. Clean off the end of the pencil with a baby wipe.

- Mix a dark pink shade of puffy paint on the palette with a toothpick. Use the sharpened end of the pencil to create the small dashes under the eyes for the blushing cheeks.

- Now teens should put on their second pair of gloves. Have each teen apply the "icing" at the top of the Popsicle. The icing color can be any color they choose. The layer should be quite thick, and it will have a bumpy appearance when it is applied. I don't care for the bumpy look, so I smooth it out gently with a gloved finger (similar to icing a cake).

- Have teens trade off with a partner to hold their Popsicle upright while they remove their gloves.

- Use sprinkles on the top icing layer (see figure 13.1 for completed squishy).

- Allow to dry for six full hours before squishing.

LEARNING OUTCOMES

Participants will . . .
- Learn the versatility of everyday materials in art making. (Oftentimes, products have more than one use [i.e., memory foam can be used for comfort during sleep or for creating an art project].)
- Experience less traditional ways of making art. (Painting with fingers and sculpting a 3-D shape with scissors are uncommon art-making techniques.)

RECOMMENDED NEXT PROJECTS

- Paint a kawaii face on a tote bag or phone case with puffy paint.
- Do a squishy makeover. Take a manufactured kawaii squishy and turn it into a completely different creature or food item with puffy paint.

Cute Needle-Felted Critters

MARY JARVIS ROBINSON
Adult Services Librarian, Novi Public Library

3-D NEEDLE FELTING is like sculpting with unspun wool. Although at first glance needle felting may seem intimidating and complicated, it's actually quite forgiving and approachable for newbies, as it has a quick learning curve, requires minimal supplies, and can be done almost anywhere. Participants can make cute and whimsical creatures in one fun session.

There are two ways to felt by hand: wet felting, where agitating wool fibers in hot water causes them to knit together permanently, and dry felting, a technique also known as needle felting. Needle felting is the art of sculpting wool with special barbed needles that enmesh wool fibers together with each punch of the needle. The more it's punched, the tighter and firmer the fibers knit together. It's a little more forgiving as well—if a mistake is made, the colors can be pulled apart, and participants can start over. Needle felting can be a 2-D format by felting wool to a flat base; it becomes 3-D when felted shapes are put together or wrapped around a freestanding armature.

Creating cute and whimsical felted animals is a fun and easy way to introduce participants to dry needle felting.

Age Range	Type of Library Best Suited For
Young adults (ages 13–18) Adults	Public libraries School libraries (middle school and high school)

Figure 14.1 | Cute needle-felted critters

Cost Estimate

The total cost for this program is about $50, which breaks down to $2.50 per person. Most materials can be purchased at a craft store and Amazon. com.

OVERVIEW

After a successful session of 2-D needle felting during Novi Public Library's Craftastic Wednesday program, attendees wanted to try their hand at 3-D needle felting. After a little research, it seemed that cute critters would be a nice starting point because the basic body shape could be used for a variety of creatures—birds, bears, frogs, and common pets. Once they understand the basic technique, participants are encouraged to do their own thing and experiment with their own design.

Because of the level of difficulty and potential of poking oneself, this class should be limited to teens and adults. Limiting it to 20 participants is manageable with just one instructor and a handout with images and step-by-step instructions. A full hour and a half is needed to get a good start on the figures. Some were able to complete a critter, whereas others took materials home to finish later.

Materials List

- Wool roving of various colors and one large roll of raw natural white
  - Wool roving, sometimes called top comb roving, means the unspun wool fibers lay in the same direction. It looks a bit like cotton candy! It can be purchased as a natural fiber or dyed into just about any color.
- Multipurpose foam
  - This can be purchased inexpensively from Home Depot. An X-Acto knife can be used to cut it down to individual sizes. We reused the foam from the bookmark (chapter 15) project.
- Styrofoam balls or eggs of various sizes (1½-inch and 2-inch diameter worked well to make a body and head).
- Craft wire to create armatures. Pipe cleaners also work well.
- Sheets of thin craft felt to make accessories, beaks, feet, and wings
- Toothpicks
- Glass eyes

Optional Materials
- Band-Aids and antibiotic cream for poked fingers
- Embroidery floss and needles to create facial features
- Fishing line
- Twigs to create arms and antlers

Necessary Equipment
- Felting needles
  - Basic 36- or 38-gauge needles are fine, one per attendee (however, have a few extras just in case some break)
- Scissors
- Glue gun with extra glue sticks

STEP-BY-STEP INSTRUCTIONS

Preparation

- If craft foam bases aren't already on hand from a previous project, they will need to be cut in advance, one of each placed at each seat.
- Place a felting needle at each seat.

- Place a length of white wool roving and a small and larger Styrofoam egg or ball at each seat. A selection of wool roving colors should be distributed at each table.
- Create sample pieces in advance to show the class a few examples of what can be made.
- If possible, create a simple handout of step-by-step instructions with images to help participants follow along with the instructor.

PROJECT INSTRUCTIONS

- This is a step-by-step guide to creating a 3-D needle-felted animal. Needle felting involves the use of sharp, barbed needles, so warn participants to be careful! It's easy to poke oneself.
- Although experienced needle felters can make amazingly realistic animals, encourage participants to start simply by making an easy, whimsical critter that has a basic body shape—like an owl, penguin, frog, or teddy bear.
- Begin by flattening one side of the Styrofoam ball or the wide end of the egg by gently pushing it down on the table. This will create a flat base for the critter.
- Begin working on the body of the critter by wrapping wool roving around the larger foam shape, then use the needle to poke it repeatedly while slowly turning the egg. Grasping the needle closer to its center will help reduce the chance of pricking fingers as the wool fibers are punched together. Vertically stab the needle through the wool into the foam. It's important to use the needle in a vertical motion because if tilted too much there is a greater risk in breaking the tip of the needle.
- As this is repeated, the surface becomes less fluffy and more fixed as the barbs on the needle catch and push the wool fibers into the base mat.
- It will take about 10–15 minutes to cover a 2- to 3-inch egg/ball.
- Occasionally, striping will appear as the wool is worked. If this happens, spread the felt evenly with the needle to dissipate the stripe, and punch it down again. More wool can be added as well.
- Lay colors over each other to add details and mix colors/tones—it's like painting with wool!
- Colors can be blended by continuously pulling apart the wool fibers of one color by hand and adding additional colors. Keep pulling apart and blending until the desired color is achieved.

- Experiment with twisting the wool fibers into a yarn-like string to create lines and definition while punching it in. Twist the fibers into little knots to create texture. Strands can remain wispy to look like fur.
- Once the body is smoothly and evenly covered with felted wool, other colors can be added to define the animal's chest and belly and to give its coat unique and colorful markings.
- A head can be made by rolling a length of wool roving into a ball or by wrapping a smaller Styrofoam shape. Like the body, stab it with the needle while slowly turning it until it is felted into a smooth, firm, round shape.
- The head is attached by using a toothpick to connect the two shapes. Then circle a length of roving around the neck and blend it to the body by grabbing a little bit of the wool on the side of the head and punching the needle all the way through the neck into the body while slowly turning the shape.
- Add features, such as paws, ears, noses, snouts, and horns, by continuously folding a ball of wool with the needle while stabbing it and shaping it until it becomes the desired shape. Leave extra wisps of wool at the end of the shape as the excess will be used to attach it to the body.
- Prominent details such as tails, wings, arms, or legs can be made with a simple wire armature constructed out of pipe cleaners or craft wire. Then wrap wool roving around the structure, adding more where definition is needed, such as in the knees and feet, and then felt it together with the needle.
- Feet and wings, as well as accessories such as a scarf, can be added by cutting shapes out of felt fabric and gluing them to the body of the critter. A mouth can be sewn on with a bit of embroidery floss. Rosy cheeks made with a bit of pink wool roving add another level of kawaii, or cuteness.
- Rub or brush the felt a little to make the shape fuzzier if you don't want the dense poke marks to show.
- Whiskers can be added to the critter with strands of fishing line or craft wire. Poke a hole with the needle where the whiskers go and glue them in place. Crinkly whiskers can be made by bending the wire. Arms and antlers can be made with twigs.
- Finally, use a dab of glue to add glass bead eyes and enjoy your cute felted critter!

LEARNING OUTCOMES

Participants will . . .

- Gain a basic understanding of the technique. (Participants may not finish in an hour and a half timeframe. The goal is for them to learn the basics of dry needle felting. If possible, let participants finish later by allowing them to take a needle and some extra wool home.)
- Understand that dry needle felting requires simple tools and easy-to-find materials and has a quick learning curve. (It is a great hobby to pick up if they are looking for something portable, hands-on, and creative.)
- Gain the skill and confidence to continue on their own and try a similar project or venture into new territory by trying complex projects, such as wearable art, wall hangings where 2-D and 3-D are combined, and amazingly realistic animals. (With time and practice, they will be able to create gorgeous works of art.)

RECOMMENDED NEXT PROJECTS

Once the basics are mastered, participants can take their craft further by making complex figures that have an armature skeleton and can stand on their own.

Cozy Needle-Felted Bookmarks

MARY JARVIS ROBINSON
Adult Services Librarian, Novi Public Library

AT A FIRST glance, needle felting may seem like a complicated craft filled with all kinds of unfamiliar (and dangerous!) tools, but participants of Novi Public Library's Craftastic Wednesday program learned a new craft and made a lovely felted bookmark in one fun session.

There are two ways to felt by hand: wet felting, where agitating wool fibers in hot water causes them to knit together permanently, and dry felting, a technique also known as needle felting. Needle felting is the art of using special barbed needles to enmesh wool fibers together with each punch of the needle. The more it's punched, the tighter and firmer the fibers knit together. It's a bit like painting with wool. Different color fiber stands are blended together to create new colors, textures, shadowing, and shapes. Needle felting can be a 2-D format by felting wool into the flat base or 3-D when felted shapes are put together or wrapped around an armature.

Bookmarks are a great way to introduce participants to the wonderful world of flat needle felting. This project will consist of needle felting with freeform designs, as well as using stencils and cookie cutters as guides. A flat felt backing is used as the canvas, and several styles of needle felting will be explored.

Age Range	Type of Library Best Suited For
Tweens (ages 8–12) Young adults (ages 13–18) Adults	Public libraries School libraries (middle school and high school)

Cost Estimate

Most materials can be purchased at a craft store such as Michaels (save up the coupons!) and Amazon.com. The estimate is about $3 per person.

OVERVIEW

This class works well for tweens, teens, and adults. Felting needles are very sharp, so it's not recommended for younger ages. Warn attendees to be careful and have a few Band-Aids on hand for poked fingers. One instructor taught the class with 20 in attendance. It worked well for the instructor to give a brief felting demonstration at the beginning of the class showing the basics as well as some advanced techniques. A handout with illustrations will help participants follow along.

Materials List

- Wool roving of various colors, one large roll of raw natural white
  - Wool roving, sometimes called top comb roving, means the unspun wool fibers lay in the same direction. You can buy it as a natural fiber or dyed into just about any color.

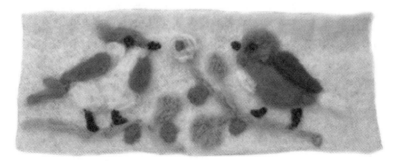

Figure 15.1 | A cozy needle-felted bookmark made by a participant

- Multipurpose foam
  - This can be purchased inexpensively from Home Depot. The foam will need to be cut down to a workable size. An X-Acto knife can be used to cut it down.
- Sheets or rolls of prefelted wool base, such as Dimensions Needlecrafts Feltworks Felt, in various colors. This can be purchased at a craft store like Michaels.
- Ribbons

Optional Materials
- Various cookie cutter shapes; simple shapes are best
- Stencils; those with larger, simple shapes like birds, daisies, and hearts work best
- Water-soluble paper
- Band-Aids and antibiotic cream on hand for poked fingers

Necessary Equipment
- Felting needles
  - Basic 36-gauge needles are fine, one per attendee. However, it's a good idea to have a few extras just in case some break.
- Scissors
- Hole punch

STEP-BY-STEP INSTRUCTIONS

Preparation

- The craft foam and prefelted wool base need to be cut to size in advance. The foam needs to be a little bigger than the bookmark. Larger (3 inches × 7 inches) than typical bookmarks should be cut so that participants have space to experiment with various techniques and shapes. Place one of each at each seat.
- Distribute a selection of wool roving colors to each table.
- The stencils and cookie cutters should be displayed in a central location so that participants can select their favorites.
- Precut ribbons of different colors.

PROJECT INSTRUCTIONS

- This is a step-by-step guide to creating a needle-felted bookmark. Needle felting involves the use of sharp, barbed needles, so warn participants to be careful! It's easy to poke oneself.
- Place the precut bookmark on the craft foam.
- Take a small pinch of wool roving and lay it onto the base fabric in the desired shape to begin making the scene. Creating simple shapes, such as hearts, flowers, animals, and landscapes, is a good way to get started. Other colors can be laid over each other to add details and mixed colors/tones—it's like painting with wool!
- Colors can be blended by continuously pulling apart the wool fiber by hand and adding in additional colors as you work it. Keep pulling apart and blending until the desired color is achieved.
- Take up the felting needle by grasping it close to its center. This will help reduce the chance of pricking a finger as the wool fibers are punched together. Vertically stab the needle through the wool, through the felt mat, and into the foam but not all the way through. It's important to use the needle in an up-and-down motion because if tilted too much, there is a greater risk in breaking off the tip of the needle.
- As this is repeated, the surface becomes less fluffy and more fixed as the barbs on the needle catch and push the wool fibers into the base mat.
- Experiment with twisting the wool fibers into a yarn-like string to create lines and definition. Twist the fibers into little knots to create texture. Strands can remain wispy to look like hair, fur, or grass.
- When finished, gently peel the felted fabric off the base. It takes some coaxing because the fibers become planted within the foam.
- Use the punch to make a hole at the top and tie on a colorful ribbon.

Additional needle felting techniques are as follows:
- With cookie cutters
  - If a participant is hesitant to try an image of their own design, encourage them to use a cookie cutter as a guide to place a 2-D shape on a precut bookmark. Popular cookie cutter shapes are hearts, stars, snowflakes, birds, cats, and dogs. The simpler the shape, the better.
  - Place the cookie cutter, sharp edge down, onto your prefelted bookmark base. Then stuff wool roving into the shape. Hold the cookie cutter while stabbing around the inner edge with the needle. Add more wool as it becomes flatter. Keep the cookie cutter in place until

the outline is completed, and then more wool can be added to fill in the shape to the desired thickness.

- With stencils
  - Stencils are a great way to embellish the bookmark with more intricate designs.
  - Like with the cookie cutters, hold the stencil over the bookmark base and fill the shape in with wool by stabbing repeatedly and evenly with the felting needle. Add more wool as needed to fill in the shape to the desired thickness.
- With water-soluble paper
  - Freestanding felted items such as decorative embellishments and jewelry (such as pendants and brooches) can be easily created with water-soluble paper placed over the felting foam board.
  - Draw or trace a shape, such as a flower or butterfly, onto water-soluble paper, and then fill it with wool and felting it through the paper. When the shape has reached its desired thickness, cut around the outline.
  - Briefly dip the paper in tepid water to dissolve it.
  - Press the shape in a towel to squeeze out the excess water. Continue to shape it into a freestanding piece by adding more wool and molding it and then letting it dry in that position. Add a fastener to the back and wear it on a coat or pinned to a bag.

LEARNING OUTCOMES

Participants will . . .

- Find that needle felting is a great hobby to pick up if looking for something hands-on and creative. (With time and practice, they can create anything from gorgeous works of art to wearable objects.)
- Find this craft to be a confidence booster for those who are uncertain about their creative talents because templates can be used to help with the design, it is forgiving, and the outcome is rewarding and attention-getting.

RECOMMENDED NEXT PROJECTS

Try 3-D felting, such as the Cute Needle-Felted Critters project in chapter 14.

Ice Cream Kawaii Felt Keychain

SEE (PAIGE) VANG

Library Associate, Saint Paul Public Library

THIS PROJECT WILL teach patrons how to hand-sew, using the blanket stitch technique, commonly seen in kawaii crafts, to create a kawaii-inspired strawberry ice cream keychain. Attendees can accessorize, so they can boost the cuteness of the keychain, either by adding additional felt or by adding tiny gems and beads to it.

Age Range
Young adults (ages 13–18)
Adults

Type of Library Best Suited For
Public libraries
School libraries

Cost Estimate

- $5–$15 (There are additional costs if particpants want to add gems/beads or if they want to make more item.)

OVERVIEW

Provide a simple pattern for attendees. The project will entail that patrons learn how to make ruffles and an attachment strap, and compile all the pieces together using the blanket stitch. The project should be planned for a

two-hour-long session, with one person to lead
and one other for assistance. The suggested
group size is six to eight people and no more,
as hand-sewing can be very time-consuming.

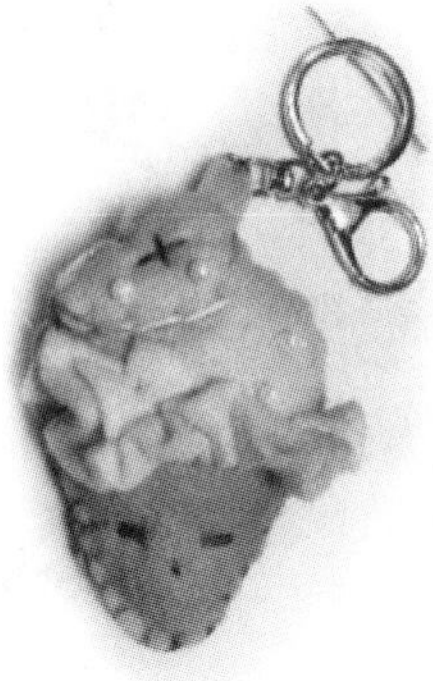

Materials List

- Pattern
- Felt in a variety of colors
- Needle
- Thread in a variety of colors
- Keychain attachment clip
- Jump ring

Figure 16.1 | Kawaii ice cream keychain

Optional Materials

- Tracing paper and pencil
- Marking tools
- Ribbon scrap
- Gems and beads

- Glue
- Scissors
- Needle and thread
- Felt

STEP-BY-STEP INSTRUCTIONS

Preparation

- Print pattern so that it's ready for use by attendees.
- Prepare scissors and utensils for cutting and marking the pattern onto the felt.
- If you have the time, it is best to have an assortment of colors, precut and ready for attendees to grab to use.
- Thread needles in a variety of color choices.

PROJECT INSTRUCTIONS

- Patrons will start the project by selecting their choice of colored felt, needle, and thread.
- Cut out all pieces using the pattern provided.
- Start with making a ruffle, and add to the edge of the cream shape. To make the ruffle, patrons will use the running stitch on the long rectangle

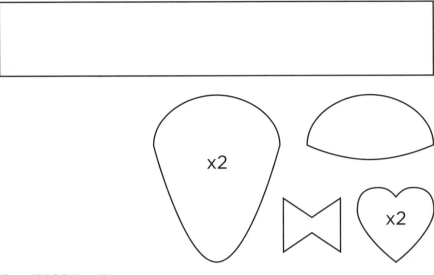

Figure 16.2 | Pattern pieces

shape and then tighten the thread. Once tightened, place on the edge of the bottom of the cream shape, and use a whip stitch to attach both pieces together.

- Next, place the two bigger shapes on top of each other, and then the cream shape with the ruffle on the first top layer. Patrons will use the blanket stitch to enclose all edges. To do a blanket stitch, start between the two big shapes on the side, and before doing the next stitch, patrons will want to loop it between the thread. Patrons will use the blanket stitch until they reach the top.
- At the very top of the cream shape, insert a small 2- to 3-inch length of felt, folded in half, and place at the top. Sew the blanket stitch on top and around the edge.
- Before you finish up your stitch, leave about 1 inch of space. Place stuffing inside, and then close it off with the blanket stitch.
- The ice cream felt keychain is done. Remember to give it eyes and a cute smile.
- To accessorize, patrons may make additional mini felt objects or glue on tiny sparkly crystals, gems, or beads.
- Once finished, patrons will use the attach loop on the ice cream felt and then on a separate keychain clip to clip together using a jump ring.

LEARNING OUTCOMES

Participants will . . .
- Learn the blanket stitch technique.
- Learn how to make a simple ruffle.
- Learn how to best accessorize a felt keychain.
- Learn simple cut-out shapes.

RECOMMENDED NEXT PROJECTS

- Make tiny felt plushies and accessorize them with jewelry and cute bows.
- Use learned techniques to make gifts such as hearts for Valentine's Day or cupcakes for birthdays.
- Use techniques for bigger felt projects and make everyday food objects.

ONLINE REFERENCES

- Blanket stitch: www.youtube.com/watch?v=S9zegUYdPmg
- Whip stitch: www.holiday-crafts-and-creations.com/whip-stitch.html

PART III

QUILLING, ORIGAMI, AND PAPER PROJECTS

Miniature Books

JESSICA FRANCO

Teen Librarian, Groton Public Library

https://jessarae020.wordpress.com/2015/03/17/read-from-your-ears/

EVERYTHING IS CUTER when it is tiny, and the same applies to books! These miniature books are the perfect craft for story-loving patrons of any library. The books can be customized to reflect the maker's interests through the choice of paper, illustrations, and text. This flexibility makes them ideal for a teen read week and other literary celebrations.

Age Range	Type of Library Best Suited For
Kids (ages 3–7) Tweens (ages 8–12) Young adults (ages 13–18) Adults	Public libraries Academic libraries School libraries

Cost Estimate

- $0–$20
- Many of the supplies are readily available in most libraries' supply closets. If not, the supplies can be purchased at reasonable prices from craft or dollar stores, as well as online.

OVERVIEW

During this program, participants will make their own
miniature book. The program
should be at least an hour,
possibly longer if the expected
participants are unfamiliar
with sewing. If possible, have
two staff members available to
answer questions and demonstrate the process as you walk
through it. Because the program is miniature, be prepared
to introduce the steps to the
group and then demonstrate

Figure 17.1 | Books can be as small as your fingertips!

at each table. This may mean having multiple samples in progress or being
able to undo and repeat steps along the way.

Materials List

Necessary Equipment

- Scissors and/or
  small paper cutter
- Pencils
- Glue
- Ruler or ruled workstation
- Thumbtacks

- Needles and thread
- Cardboard (cereal or snack boxes
  work great)
- Paper (decorative and/or plain)
- Pens and markers for adding
  content

STEP-BY-STEP INSTRUCTIONS

Preparation

- Set up supply trays with the supplies and materials needed to create a
  book. Each participant should have a needle, thread, thumbtack, and
  cardboard.
- Give each table pencils, glue, scissors, and rulers. If you are offering
  scrapbook or patterned paper for the decorative covers, give each table
  a sampling of the options.

- Cutting to size: Depending on the age group, you may want to cut the paper to size ahead of time (see the project instructions for exact measurements). This will help save time and give more time for sewing the binding.

PROJECT INSTRUCTIONS

- Welcome the group to the program and introduce the craft. Show an example of a finished book and give a brief overview of how they will get there.
- Give participants a chance to browse any decorative paper and choose their colors.
- Walk participants through the following steps. As you do, create a book with them so they can see each step demonstrated.
  - Cutting the Cardboard
    » Using a piece of cardboard, measure and cut a rectangle of 1 × 1¾ inches. Be sure to get a straight line by using a paper cutter or ruler.
  - Creating a Fold Line
    » Next, measure and draw a line down the center of each cover.
    » Draw and score two lines next to the center line, approximately ¹/₁₆ inch away.
    » Create a fold line by gently folding the cardboard along the outside lines, leaving the middle as the spine.
  - Preparing the Paper
    » Measure and cut five to eight pieces of paper; these will be the pages of your book. The paper should measure ¾ × 1½ inches. The number of pieces you cut will determine the thickness of your book. The thicker the book, the more challenging the sewing step will be; anyone new to sewing should be encouraged to try a thinner book first.
    » Fold the pile in half, making a crease in the paper.
    » While folded, cut the edges so they are even.
  - Preparing the Binding
    » Lay the stack of paper on the cardboard cover and align the papers' creases to the center line.
    » Using the thumbtack, poke three holes into the paper and cover.

- Stitching the Binding
    - » Thread a needle with string and tie a knot at the end.
    - » Stitch down through the top hole, leaving the knot inside the book. Stitch up through the middle hole and back down through the bottom. Bring the needle back through the middle and repeat the process until the binding is secure.
    - » This is the most complicated step, so be sure to save stitches for demonstrating at each table.
    - » When you finish, tie a knot with the excess thread by looping through the stitches against the back spine.
- Cutting the Cover
    - » Cut a rectangle out of colored paper or cardstock that is 3¼ inches wide and 2 inches long. This will be the decorative dust jacket.
    - » Center the newly finished book on the decorative paper and trace the shape onto the dust jacket. Keep the book and paper together in case there are minor differences in sizing.
- Creating Flaps for the Dust Jacket
    - » Draw lines from the corners of your traced rectangle to the edge of the paper. This should make small trapezoids on the sides of your rectangle.
    - » Trim off the corners based on your lines.
    - » Mark the edges of the spine on the top and bottom of the dust jacket. Cut out the space in between the lines.
    - » Once cut, create fold lines to give the flaps a little flexibility.
- Attaching the Cover
    - » Apply a healthy amount of glue to the rectangle, taking care that you are using the backside of the paper.
    - » Press the cover firmly into the glue.
    - » Apply glue to the top and bottom flaps, and then fold them over onto the cover. Be sure that you move the pages out of the way as you do this.
    - » Next, glue the side flaps, covering the remaining cardboard and parts of the top/bottom flaps.
- Adding Content
    - » Using a medium of your choice, fill your pages with text or illustrations for a true miniature book.

Figure 17.2 | The dust jacket will have flaps that fold over the cover.

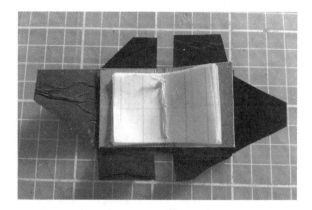

- As participants finish, have them share their miniature books with each other: Why did they choose certain paper? What did they add for content? And so on.
- Take photos of participants with their books or of the miniature books with library books to share on the patron's or the library's social media.

LEARNING OUTCOMES

Participants will . . .
- Understand the process of creating a physical book.
- Learn to take detailed measurements on a small scale.
- Learn to use their sewing skills to create the binding of a book.

RECOMMENDED NEXT PROJECTS

The miniature books can be kept as adorable keepsakes or modified to become jewelry. Wrapping a little jewelry wire or eye pin around the binding will prepare the book for becoming a pendant or even an earring. This can be done before or after gluing on the dust jacket. Libraries can also challenge participants to come up with new measurements, seeing who can make the smallest book. This is a great way to incorporate mathematics into your program, thus supporting educational standards and curriculum.

Kawaii Paper Squishy

MARISSA LIEBERMAN
Children's Librarian, East Orange Public Library

CHILDREN AND TEENS will create their very own cute stuffed squishies made from paper, tape, and paper towels. Squishy patterns can include kawaii sushi, smiling fruit, or a colored rectangle with a smiley face on it.

Age Range	Type of Library Best Suited For	Cost Estimate
Tweens (ages 8–12)	Public libraries	$0

OVERVIEW

A paper squishy is a free and simple stuffed craft project made with common items and requires no prior knowledge. Rather than needle and thread, paper squishies are "sewed" together using tape or a stapler. Patrons can design and color their paper in a variety of ways. Paper squishies can be stuffed with whatever soft material you have on hand. At my library, we always have paper towels around. To laminate the squishies, making them sturdier, put clear tape over the squishies. Paper squishies can work as a formal or self-directed program. Looking to add more STEAM components? Make a light-up squishy using paper circuits or combine with a slime workshop. Instead of paper towels, place slime inside a Ziploc bag and stuff inside the squishy.

Materials List

- Paper
- Stuffing: paper towels/
  tissues/plastic bags
- Book/shipping tape

- Stapler
- Scissors
- Markers/crayons
- Sample

Optional Materials

- Coin cell battery
  (to add a paper circuit element)
- Copper tape
  (to add a paper circuit element)

- 5-millimeter LED light
  (to add a paper circuit element)
- Slime inside Ziploc bag
  (for slime "stuffing")

STEP-BY-STEP INSTRUCTIONS

Preparation

- Gather materials and place on tables.

PROJECT INSTRUCTIONS

- For the easiest squishy, fold your paper in half bottom to top. For more
  advanced squishies, cut your paper into a triangle or another shape.
  Keep in mind that as with sewing a pattern, both sides should be exactly
  the same.

- Color/decorate your squishy.
- Tape the edges closed, leaving an opening at the top. If you have a more complicated shape, it may be easier to staple the edges closed.
- Rip paper towels into strips and crumple them up.
- Stuff into your paper squishy.
- Tape the top closed.
- To laminate, cover the back and front of the squishy with large strips of clear tape.

LEARNING OUTCOMES

Participants will . . .
- Gain a basic understanding of sewing principles through this no-sew project.
- Learn to use everyday items to create a cute, finished product.

RECOMMENDED NEXT PROJECTS

- Slime squishy
- Paper circuit light-up squishy
- Binder squishy
- Felties

19

Monster/Emoji Bookmarks

CHRISTINA DUFOUR
Young Adult Librarian, Thayer Public Library

SO YOU'RE READING your new book and you realize you're missing something—your bookmark! But have no fear, you can make one quickly and easily with a few steps, your paper of choice, and some markers or colored pencils you have lying around. You can teach library patrons of all ages how to create these in so many ways. They are a fun project and are ideal for gifts, book clubs, or school book sales.

Age Range	Type of Library Best Suited For
Kids (ages 3–7) Tweens (ages 8–12) Young adults (ages 13–18) Adults	Public libraries Academic libraries School libraries

Cost Estimate

- $0–$20
- Many of the supplies are readily available in most libraries' supply closets. If not, the supplies can be purchased at reasonable prices from craft or dollar stores, as well as online.

OVERVIEW

During this program, participants will make their own
monster origami bookmarks
(alternatively, depending on
the desire and skill of the participant, they could also make
emoji or animal/character kawaii
bookmarks). The program can be
paired easily with other papercraft activities and will take
anywhere from 20 minutes to
one hour. It all depends on how
detailed participants want to get.

Figure 19.1 | Growl!

Having a printed set of steps is helpful, as you will likely be going from table
to table to demonstrate various parts of the folding process. But once participants catch on, it really takes off.

Materials List

Necessary Equipment

- Scissors
- Pencils
- Colored pencils
- Markers
- Glue
- Rulers

- Paper (decorative
  and/or plain,
  scrapbook paper,
  or construction
  paper is also OK)
- Glue gun (optional)

- Googly eyes
  (optional)
- Decorative items:
  pipe cleaners, feath-
  ers, glitter, and so on
  (optional)

STEP-BY-STEP INSTRUCTIONS

Preparation

- Set up tables with the supplies and materials needed to create a bookmark. Add a general spread of the above equipment.
- On each table, provide markers, colored pencils, pencils, glue, scissors,
  and rulers. If you decide to use googly eyes, pipe cleaners, or other
  optional crafting items, also provide a sampling of those. If you are

offering special paper, like scrapbook or patterned paper, give each table a few sheets of those as well.

- If you decide to print an instructional packet, make sure each table has at least one copy.

PROJECT INSTRUCTIONS

- Welcome the group to the program and introduce the craft. Show an example of some finished monster or emoji bookmarks and any other crafts they will be trying.
- Give participants a chance to pick their seats and browse the items provided at each table.
- Walk participants through the following steps. As you do, create an origami bookmark with them.
  - Cutting the Paper
    » Using a piece of paper, ruler, and a pencil, cut a square that is 6 × 6 inches. Optional for monster or animal: using a separate piece of paper of another color (preferably solid), make a slightly less than 3 × 3 inches square. Set this aside.
  - Creating the Folds
    » With the large square, fold the bottom to the top so that you have a triangle.
    » Fold the left corner and the right corner to the center point.
    » Open your triangle.
    » Fold the top flap of the center to the bottom.
    » Take the left corner and right corner and tuck them into the middle "pocket." This creates the base for your bookmark.
  - Decorating Your Monster/Emoji Bookmark
    » This is where participants get to have fun and let their imagination play. They can make shark teeth, wavy teeth, green eyes, a purple nose, googly eyes, a curly tail, or whatever they'd like to add to their monster. When they've finished, the bookmark is ready to start using!
- As participants finish, have them share their creations: Did they name their monster? Why did they choose a certain emoji or a certain paper? What additional pieces were they required to cut to design their bookmark? And so on.

Figure 19.2 | Let's get
ready to fold!

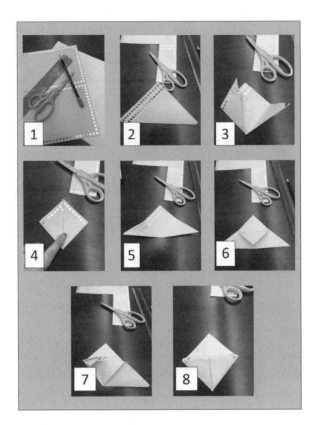

- Take photos of
participants
with their
bookmarks and
maybe with
library books
to share on the
patron's or the
library's social
media.

LEARNING OUTCOMES

Participants will . . .
- Understand the process of creating simple origami.
- Learn to take detailed measurements for folding.
- Learn to use their imagination and get creative.

RECOMMENDED NEXT PROJECTS

Turn this into a volunteer activity/program. Have your teens make a bunch of these and then donate them to your children's department to give with library cards or to be used for a future program. These would also make great promotional pieces for a farmers' market or other event your library has a table for. Teens often need volunteer hours and many of them enjoy being creative, so this is a natural blending of the two and gives them an easy way to give back to the community.

20

Paper Roses

ASHLEY NICHOLE SIMS

Teen Services Library Assistant, Louisville Free Public Library

THESE ROSES LOOK fantastic but are so simple to make. They look fancy enough to hang up as décor in your house but are so easy that you can teach children to make them in just a few steps—which makes them a perfect library program!

Age Range	Type of Library Best Suited For
Tweens (ages 8–12) Young adults (ages 13–18) Adults	Public libraries School libraries

Cost Estimate

- $0–$10
- There's likely no need for you to spend any money on this project because your library probably already has everything, but you could buy nice paper if you're feeling fancy.

OVERVIEW

This is a fairly simple craft, but it's just complex enough that I would supervise it, especially with younger patrons so they don't get discouraged.

These roses can be scaled up easily into very large roses that would make interesting wall art; the size of your spiral and paper determines the size of your rose.

Materials List

- Construction paper (or similarly colorful, semistiff paper)
- Liquid glue

Figure 20.1 | Completed paper rose

Necessary Equipment
- Scissors
- Marker or pen

STEP-BY-STEP INSTRUCTIONS

Preparation

With younger patrons, you may want to draw the spirals for them ahead of time.

PROJECT INSTRUCTIONS

- Draw a spiral with a blunt end on your paper.
- Cut out the spiral inside your line so the line will be hidden on the bottom of the rose.
- Starting from the blunt end, roll up the paper tightly.
- Once you've rolled everything, let it relax and arrange your rose.
- Put a dab of glue in the bottom center to secure your petals.
- Optionally, you can cut out leaves and glue them to the bottom.

LEARNING OUTCOMES

Participants will . . .

- Learn a simple papercraft that can be remixed by sizing up or using different kinds of paper.
- Make something 3-D and beautiful with very little effort (this could be a big confidence booster for kids looking to try complex origami forms).

RECOMMENDED NEXT PROJECTS

- Other paper flower projects can be added so your patrons can make a whole bouquet!
- This project pairs well with paper-folding (origami) and quilling projects.
- Because this can be scaled up to a home décor project, other décor projects or wall art projects are recommended.

21

Paper Fortune Cookies

ASHLEY NICHOLE SIMS

Teen Services Library Assistant, Louisville Free Public Library

LET'S BE CLEAR: First and foremost, fortune cookies are not Chinese. Even though most Chinese takeout will come packaged with fortune cookies, they are certainly not a traditional Chinese dessert by any stretch of the imagination. They most likely came from Japanese immigrants to the United States and were adopted by Chinese restaurants to adapt to American tastes. A short talk about this little-known history would be easy to deliver while you make these with your patrons.

Paper fortune cookies are a fun and surprisingly simple craft that gives an opportunity for discussion of how real fortune cookies are made and where they came from. These could be premade with fortunes for a quick giveaway for younger kids and are a simple all-ages craft that can be done last minute with supplies already in your library.

Age Range	Type of Library Best Suited For
Kids (ages 3–7) Tweens (ages 8–12) Young adults (ages 13–18) Adults	Public libraries Academic libraries School libraries

Cost Estimate

- $0–$10
- It is likely you have all the required materials already in your library, but some patterned origami paper would be a fun type of paper to use.

OVERVIEW

The way the paper is folded here is the exact same way the dough is folded in fortune cookies. This project is so simple that I've left it up as a passive program in my teen section with examples, supplies, and a sign explaining the steps. This is a *very* low-stress craft.

Materials List

- Paper (it's good to have color and pattern options)
- Glue sticks (or tape in a pinch)

Necessary Equipment

- Printer (for fortunes)
- Scissors

STEP-BY-STEP INSTRUCTIONS

Preparation

- For younger patrons, it might be good to draw or cut circles beforehand.
- Print out a list of fortunes and make up your own! Look online for inspiration if you're stuck. Offer patrons the list, and let them make up their own; funny fortunes can be one of the best parts of this program.

PROJECT INSTRUCTIONS

- Cut a circle out of your paper.
- Apply glue (or tape) on middle of the side you want facing outward.
- Fold the circle in half, but do not crease it.
- Hold the paper on the outside edges and press in the middle to bring the edges together.

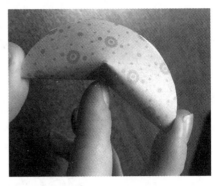

Figure 21.1 | Paper fortune cookie

Figure 21.2 | First fold of the fortune cookie

- Hold the edges for a few seconds to make sure the glue/tape holds.
- Cut out a fortune and stick it into one side of your cookie. With paper cookies, I like to leave an edge peeking out instead of folding the fortune inside so they can be easily tugged free without tearing the paper.

LEARNING OUTCOMES

Participants will . . .
- Learn the surprising history behind fortune cookies.
- Develop fine motor skills through the slightly tricky folding maneuver (younger participants).
- Learn how fortune cookies are made.

RECOMMENDED NEXT PROJECTS

- This project would be great to pair with the Jar of Stars project in chapter 22, which is also simple paper folding and Japanese in origin.
- Once patrons have done this project, other forms of paper folding will probably be on their horizon. I recommend having a few origami books ready for patrons to page through.

Jar of Stars

CHANTALE PARD

Youth Services Librarian, Keshen Goodman Public Library

JAR OF STARS sees creators using small, decorative strips of paper to fold into tiny, puffy stars. This is a versatile project for a variety of budgets—you can keep it at no cost if you're using in-house office supplies and recycled bottles, or you can spend a few dollars on a cute-shaped glass jar and some pretty holographic foil strips. Either way, the simplicity and miniature size of these lucky stars are sure to keep things kawaii!

This activity can be a great team-building activity and can even have elements of mindfulness and meditation in the focused nature of these repetitive movements.

Age Range	Type of Library Best Suited For	Cost Estimate
Tweens (ages 8–12) Young adults (ages 13–18)	Public libraries School libraries	$0–$20

OVERVIEW

Whenever I've run a lucky star folding activity, we've worked together as a group to try to fill a collective jar. In our monthly teen anime club meetings, our regular attendees would always start the program by folding a few stars for the jar, with the goal to have it full by the end of the school year. We also used this as a welcoming gift—teens who were new to the club were allowed to choose a lucky star from our tin to take home as a sign of our new friendship.

This activity could also fill an entire program—put on some fun background music, divide attendees into teams, and have them race to see who can fill their respective jars first within the given time limit (understanding that this way might throw the relaxation portion out the window).

Alternatively, give each attendee their own bottle to try to fill—if they don't succeed, they can continue their work when they take their project home. It is said that one can make a wish on their lucky stars if they make 100!

Materials List

- Paper strips (½ × 11 inches is ideal but can be scaled up for larger sizes by using a 1:13 ratio)
  - Paper options are limitless: plain white, colored printer paper, pages from discarded manga or a favorite novel, or even patterned paper color-printed from the Internet (try Googling "printable lucky star strips").
- A recycled clear bottle or jar or perhaps an old tea tin

Figure 22.1 | Our anime club lucky star tea tin

– One larger receptacle should do for a group project, but be sure to gather enough for all participants if they will be working toward their own take-home collection.

Optional Materials

- Lucky star paper (which can be purchased online and in a variety of craft stores or Asian gift shops/grocery stores and often comes in a variety of rainbow, glitter, or foiled holographic designs)
- Heart-, moon-, or star-shaped clear glass jars (which can also often be purchased from the same venues as the preportioned papers noted above)
- Patterned origami paper
- Card stock
- Ribbons

Necessary Equipment

- Scissors
- Hole punch
- Markers

STEP-BY-STEP INSTRUCTIONS

Preparation

Collect materials and equipment
- Precut paper strips or purchase foil lucky star folding papers.
- Purchase glass jars or gather recycled bottles/tea tins.
- Print off visual instruction sheets and have multiple copies available: Many versions of these can be found online and are also often included on the back of the lucky star paper packs.
- Prefold a few sample stars.
- Gather interesting origami facts for FYIs during folding time.

PROJECT INSTRUCTIONS

- Have participants select their folding paper—if you have a limited amount of purchased foil strips, think about putting out plain white paper versions for people who want to practice their folding techniques first.

- Younger hands often have a hard time with the pinching portion at the end of the instructions—this is the bit that takes the star from flat to puffy. Be prepared to help younger attendees with this portion of the instructions.
- If using an old tea tin as a star receptacle, think about covering it in a collage of patterned origami paper or having someone label it as a "Wishing Jar."

Figure 22.2 | Foil lucky star folding paper with visible folding instructions

- Glass jars and plastic bottles can also get label tags—use a square of cardstock to label your jar ("Lucky Stars," "Dreams," "Ava's Wishes," etc.) by hole-punching the label and tying it to the spout of the jar with a pretty ribbon.

LEARNING OUTCOMES

Participants will . . .
- Use their sequencing and fine-motor skill while following visual and textual instructions.
- Learn about the cultural history of origami.
- Learn ways to recycle old books/manga.
- Learn the importance of sharing and teamwork.

RECOMMENDED NEXT PROJECTS

- Try using pastel colored paper for a *konpeito* (Japanese star candy) look. You can even glue some googly eyes on a black pom-pom in order to recreate the soot-sprite feeding scene from *Spirited Away*. You can even check chapter 48, Neko Atsume Fluffies, to learn how to make pom-poms.
- Gather a needle and thread, and lace them through your lucky stars for an adorable tiny bunting! It looks super kawaii wrapped around a mini tree.

23

Heart Terrarium Paper Quilling, Jewelry

SEE (PAIGE) VANG

Library Associate, Saint Paul Public Library

THIS WILL TEACH library patrons of all ages the basic skills of easy quilling, to enhance their craft skills, and to create adorable, wearable tiny earrings.

Age Range	Type of Library Best Suited For	Cost Estimate
Kids (ages 3–7) Tweens (ages 8–12) Young adults (ages 13–18) Adults	Public libraries Academic libraries School libraries	$5 or less

OVERVIEW

Patrons will learn to quill simple kawaii heart and leaf shapes in order to make into a pair of earrings.

Figure 23.1 | Heart terrarium earrings

Materials List
- Cardstock paper, in the colors you would like to use and cut to size, all ¼-inch width with lengths of 8½ inches (2) and 4¼ inches (3)
- Glue
- Toothpick
- Two to four jumper rings
- Two earring hooks

Optional Materials
- Ruler
- Tweezers
- Pliers
- Scissors or paper cutter board
- Purchase precut paper quilling

STEP-BY-STEP INSTRUCTIONS
Preparation
- Precut a variety of sheets of card stock color papers to different lengths.
- Prep glue in small containers.

PROJECT INSTRUCTIONS

- First, gather the paper materials, which should be cut to size, all ¼-inch width with lengths of 8½ inches (four) and 4¼ inches (six).
- Cut out four hearts about 1 inch long.
- For the quilling, patrons can do freehand style or use a toothpick. To freehand, patrons will roll up the paper strip and glue the end piece. To use with a toothpick, patrons will wrap the paper on the toothpick and then glue. Once dried, patrons will crease the edge to make a leaf shape on all the colors, except the pink strip, leave circle as is.
- Gather all quill pieces, and first glue the leaves together. Then place on top of the bigger circle (pink strip) and glue the edge.
- While it is placed, glue the heart shape on top of the circle quill, then flip and glue the second heart on the back.
- Once dry, attach the earring hooks and craft together using a jump ring.
- Draw a smiling kawaii face using a marker, and then you are finished.

LEARNING OUTCOMES

Participants will . . .
- Learn easy quilling using a freehand style or a toothpick.
- Create papercraft earrings.

RECOMMENDED NEXT PROJECTS

- Use the quilling technique to make other jewelry types, such as a bracelet and necklace.
- Use quilling to make paper art, and gift it to friends and family.

24

Light Up Your Artwork with Paper Circuitry

MARY JARVIS ROBINSON

Adult Services Librarian, Novi Public Library

TAKE YOUR ARTWORK to new levels by lighting it up with paper circuits. A paper circuit is a functioning electronic circuit constructed on a flat piece of paper rather than on a traditional circuit board. Creating one involves using some kind of conductive material, such as copper tape, energy-efficient LEDs, and a power source such as a coin cell battery. The energy efficiency and low temperature of LEDs as compared to regular light bulbs make it possible to work on something as ephemeral as paper. Besides the low cost of this project, the beauty of paper circuits is that the "magic" lies flatly underneath your 2-D image and adds a definite wow factor to anyone's artwork. The added bonus of this project is that participants will gain a better understanding of how a basic electrical circuit works. Although this appeals to all ages, including adults, it is also great for youth STEAM programming.

Age Range	Type of Library Best Suited For
Tweens (ages 8–12) Young adults (ages 13–18) Adults	Public libraries School libraries

Cost Estimate

- Estimated to be about $1.65 per person
- Most supplies can be purchased on Amazon.com.

OVERVIEW

If this paper circuitry program is offered for youth, plan to be available for hands-on assistance. If possible, have a few teen volunteers help out. Difficulties can occur when peeling the paper backing on the copper adhesive tape, and, if it touches itself, it's extremely hard to recover. Also, even though bulbs are easier to handle than SMD (surface

Figure 24.1 | Participant painting lit up with paper circuits

mount device) LEDs, it can still be hard for youth to figure out the polarity (positive or negative) orientation. SMD LEDs are very small and hard to handle (tweezers will help), so it's also difficult to determine their positive/negative side, making it necessary to create a simple circuit test board in advance. Therefore, it's not recommended to use SMD LEDs for youth or tweens.

At least an hour will be needed to cover all aspects of the program—providing information about how electrical circuits work, creating a collage, drawing or painting, and then making and lighting it up with paper circuits. If you have sufficient volunteers on hand, it's doable to open it up to 20–30 participants.

Materials List

Most art-making materials can be found in a well-stocked supply closet. Circuitry items can be purchased through Amazon.com.

- Paper—a thicker paper will be needed if paints are used
- Drawing materials—paints, colored pencils, crayons, or markers
- Collage-making materials—old magazines, books (discarded picture books are great for this!), scrapbook paper, Mod Podge, and foam or paintbrushes

- LED lights—either SMD or 3- to 5-millimeter LED bulbs
  - Use assorted colors. Please note that while the bulbs are easier to handle, they aren't completely flat and will raise the paper, causing a bump.
- Copper foil tape
- Clear plastic tape
- Coin/button battery (CR2032 lithium metal 3V)
- Scissors

Optional Materials

- Craft foam sheets
- Tweezers for handling tiny SMD LEDs
- Pin
- Black electrical tape

STEP-BY-STEP INSTRUCTIONS

Preparation

- It is helpful to show a diagram of a simple circuit demonstrating how electrical currents work. This can be found on Google Images.
- Create a simple circuit test board in advance to make sure the lights work and to check its polarity orientation; this is especially helpful with tiny SMD LEDs.
- Create some sample pieces in advance.
- Place sheets of paper and all circuitry materials—a length of copper tape, LED, and a coin battery—at each seat. It's helpful to place the circuitry materials in cups to keep them contained because the LEDs are small and can be easily misplaced. Participants can share drawing/painting materials from a single location if there aren't enough for each table.

PROJECT INSTRUCTIONS

- Give a quick overview of how a simple circuit works, and review the materials involved.
- Have participants draw, paint, or collage a picture of something they'd like to light up. Some examples are a campfire, sunset, moonlight, stars, a firefly, a flower, and a porch light on a house at night. It's also fun to

light up greeting and holiday cards. If cards are made, fold the paper in half and the circuit will be on a separated half sheet of paper that will be glued or taped to the back of the card's cover.

- This is a good time to introduce some art-making techniques such as collage or watercolor basics.
- Once the light source is determined in the artwork, lay it over the blank sheet of paper that will contain the circuitry.
- Make a small pin-prick through the cover to the second (blank) page to indicate the spot to be lit up. The pin-prick can be marked with a pencil or pen so it can be found easily. Set the artwork aside.
- Determine and make a mark where you'd like the battery to be placed. If you'd like a small "press me" button on the cover page, a discreet bottom corner is usually best unless it's incorporated into the artwork.
- Lay down the conductive tape circuit by gently peeling off the paper backing. It can overlap itself if smaller pieces are easier to handle. It can be placed in parallel lines, which is good for adding multiple light sources, or spread apart, which is good for younger participants who may not be as careful about keeping the tape from touching or crossing. However, both lines need to lead to the battery. The circuit will not work if the tape touches!
- Select the LED light color of choice. If bulbs are used, separate the prongs, and tape (use the plastic tape) them over the pin-prick mark and have each wire lead to one side of the battery through the copper tape path. Take note of which side is the longest wire (positive). Make a + mark to identify it.
- **Please note:** It's harder to determine the polarity of SMD LEDs. Some have a small green (-) mark to indicate the negative lead, but some are not marked at all. Unfortunately, standardization hasn't been established among manufacturers and therefore it is difficult to determine the polarity orientation of SMD LEDs. The best way to check its polarity is by testing it on a simple, handmade test circuit board.
- Complete the circuit by connecting the LED to the battery with the copper conductive tape. The top side of the battery is positive (look for the +) and needs to lead to the positive prong of the LED. The wire prongs of the LED must be in contact with copper tape—the lines can't touch or cross over each other or the circuit won't work. If it doesn't work, just flip the battery and try it again. Nonconductive plastic tape can cross over the copper tape.

- Use a bit of plastic tape on the edges of the battery to hold it on the paper, but don't cover where the copper tape needs to lie or the circuit will be broken.
- For a switch, you can either fold a corner of paper so that the tape connecting the positive side of the LED comes in contact with the positive side of the battery (this connection will turn on the light) or you can keep the + line of the tape a little longer and fold it over the battery to create a simple battery switch. A pressure switch can be created by placing a doughnut-shaped piece of sheet craft foam over the coin battery. This creates enough separation that the light turns off when the cutout center isn't pressed.
- Place the artwork over the light source. If the paper is too thick, a small hole can be made over the light to allow it to shine brighter. Tape the artwork and the paper circuit together, or finish off the piece by framing it with black electrical tape.
- Make a small "press me" button with paper or craft foam over the area where the battery rests. Turn on the light(s) and enjoy your enhanced artwork!

LEARNING OUTCOMES

Participants will . . .
- Gain a hands-on understanding of how a simple circuit works.
- Be able to enhance their artwork in unique ways that will impress their friends.
- Be inspired to try to make artistic circuits in other applications, such as wearable art, and on 3-D forms by using other conductive formats beyond tape and wire, such as conductive paint, thread, and fabric.

RECOMMENDED NEXT PROJECTS

- If participants enjoyed lighting up their artwork, encourage them to try it in other artistic endeavors, such as comic art or illustrating their diary or bullet journal.
- As a next step, participants can incorporate programmed microcontrollers to make the lights in their artwork blink, flicker, or respond to sound and light through sensors.

PART IV

3-D PRINTING PROJECTS

25

Decora Hair Barrettes

OLIVIA HORVATH

Digital Services Specialist, Prince George's County Memorial Library System

EXPLORE THE HISTORY of kawaii culture, introduce 3-D printing, and make a cute and colorful takeaway during this quick and easy project perfect for tweens! Taking inspiration from "Decora" Japanese street style, participants will combine their first 3-D print with crafting materials to make freaky-fun hair accessories to wear and share. Hair clips are only half the fun—this project can be done with pin backs for flair accessible to all fashion-forward participants.

Age Range	Type of Library Best Suited For
Tweens (ages 8–12)	Public libraries Academic libraries School libraries

Cost Estimate

- $20
- The cost estimate of this project varies widely depending on what materials are being used and what filament is available for use. A version of this project using a single new color of filament, recycled crafting materials, and a few colors of paint pens and small hair clips might cost $20–$50, whereas a version of this project using multiple new colors of filament, an assortment of crafting materials in different colors, and large clips might cost $80–$150. Estimates do not include the price of a 3-D printer.

OVERVIEW

You may not know the phrase "Decora," but chances are you've seen its influence in fashion, art, and kawaii culture. "Decora" literally comes from the word "decorated," describing a subcategory of Japanese street fashion that grew out of the Lolita fashion craze of the late 1990s. Inspired by fashion icons such as Tomoe Shinohara and Kyary Pamyu Pamyu, Decora looks often share a silhouette with Lolita fashion. But where the classic Lolita ensemble emulates a dark Victorian "dolly" look, Decora's influence comes from the pastel palette of 1990's toy culture. Decora's key characteristic is an absolute excess of accessories—stuffed toys pinned to tutus, bracelet upon bracelet of candy-colored beads, chains of cartoon children's purses, and dozens of colorful hairclips snapped into just-as-colorful hair! Decora's celebration of excess is a great guiding philosophy for a playful and experimental project such as this one. In this craft, there's no such thing as "too much." As long as participants are having fun, the busier and brighter their creations look, the better!

This project is optimized for a two-hour period, for 10–15 participants and two staff members. Having one staff member aggregate and optimize files for 3-D printing while the other assists with the crafting element will keep participants engaged and on-task. The project can be run for two one-hour sessions over two days if only one staff member is available.

This project circumvents one of the biggest challenges with 3-D printer workshops—the problem of print times. By keeping the actual prints made during the workshop small (and only one part of a finished product), librarians and participants can maximize time spent experimenting and spend less on waiting around for the 3-D printer to do its thing. Keeping prints super small and simple also minimizes the chance of printer error and disappointment on behalf of participants.

Figure 25.1 | Completed decora barrettes

Materials List

- 3-D printer filament
  - PLA is recommended for safety and cost purposes. This project can be done with any color or finish of filament—pastels, bright colors, and glitter filaments are especially fun. This would be a great project to experiment with new colors or sample packs offered by some suppliers.
- Barrettes or hair clips
  - Provide participants with a few of each. For the purposes of this article, flat, "snap"-style clips between 2 and 4 inches were used. The larger clips are easier to glue on, whereas smaller clips can be made quicker and exchanged between participants. Pin backs can also be used for those who would like to prefer to wear their creations on a jacket or backpack.
- Scissors
- Glue guns
- Paint pens for coloring hair clips and 3-D prints
- 3-D printed materials
  - You will want to start the workshop with some 3-D printed pieces already printed in different sizes and colors. Simple shapes such as circles, triangles, letters, teardrops, and hearts can transform into candy-colored cats, creepy-cute eyeballs, cool characters, or fantastic abstract compositions when grouped together. This is a great way to recycle failed 3-D prints as well!
- Crafting materials
  - Foam shapes, ribbons, lace, pom-poms, buttons, feathers, die-cut confetti, fabric scraps, and other craft materials can be used behind or on top of 3-D printer pieces to add texture and pizzazz. This project is a good way to clear out scraps from past projects or breathe new life into recycled materials.

Necessary Equipment

- 3-D printer
  - This project was created using Ultimaker printers and Cura print software but can be applied to any 3-D printer and software combination. For libraries on a budget, a 3-D pen could also be substituted.
- Computers with Internet access
  - Ideally, there will be one for each participant and one operated by a staff member running the 3-D print software. It is helpful to have

the staff computer's screen projected or on a whiteboard where it is visible by participants, but that is not necessary.

STEP-BY-STEP INSTRUCTIONS

Set the Scene

- Before the workshop, generate a Tinkercad student approval code using Autodesk's Teacher tools (www.tinkercad.com/teach). This will enable you to approve the accounts of students ages 12 and under and give you the ability to download all participants' work from your account. You will also want to play around with your 3-D printer to come up with the ideal scale for your participants' projects.
- To set up workspace for the project, set out premade 3-D prints, crafting materials, clips, glue, and scissors away from where computers will be used. In a separate space, establish a digital tools-only space with 3-D printer and student computers.

Try Tinkercad! (15–20 Minutes)

- Begin the project with participants at computers. Once the crafting space is activated, it's hard to bring attention elsewhere.
- Introduce participants to the scope of the project by passing around preprinted 3-D objects and sample barrettes. Sample objects should be thin, simple shapes with a flat plane ideal for gluing to. These can be shapes you've made, premade shapes from Tinkercad, or free-to-use prints from Thingiverse.
- Guide participants through creating AutoCAD accounts, using your student approval code. Have them complete the first few Tinkercad assignments (Place It, View It, Move It, and Rotate It) so they have a grasp of the workplane and basic tools. Most participant questions can be answered by returning to these tutorials. These shouldn't take more than 5–10 minutes.

Create a Shape! (15–40 Minutes)

- Once participants have finished tutorials, lead them in creating a shape of their own. Participants can use Tinkercad's premade shapes and "doodle" function to create an abstract or recognizable design that can be printed on a small scale. Challenge participants to keep their prints to a set scale. Prints no higher than 5 millimeters (⅛ inch) work best, and because these prints need to be done before the end of the project, I recommend keeping them to as few layers as possible. My ideal scale for this project is 30 × 20 × 3 millimeters max. On your printer, choose a scale that produces prints in roughly five minutes.

- If learners are feeling challenged to come up with a shape, the emoji keyboard is a great place to start! Weather/astronomical shapes, such as clouds, sun/moon, lightning bolts, planets; silly faces (using the hole tool for eyes and mouths); alien smileys; food, such as grapes, ice cream cones, or fruits; flowers; numbers; letters; and keyboard symbols are all simple, fun, and legible at this scale.

- As participants finish their shapes, access them through your computer and output them for print. Print with 0 percent infill, no supports, and at the lowest resolution possible for lightning-fast prints. It is faster to print each file separately, as participants finish their prints, than to print in batches. If being held over two days, this will conclude the first day of the project. Participants will return to their finished 3-D prints at the start of the next session.

Get Making! (30–60 Minutes)

- While their projects are at the printer, participants may begin creating their barrettes. The theme of their shape can guide the creation of their barrette, or they may choose to lean into the Decora spirit and bring together disparate shapes, colors, and patterns to make something as crazy as it is cute.

- Guide participants to think about the larger shape of their barrette before they focus on color. The barrettes and larger craft materials will stick together best before paint pens are used. Once larger materials are glued together, participants can use paint pens and then add details that would be harder to paint around.

Bring It All Together (15–30 Minutes)

- One by one, participants will receive their finished 3-D printed shapes and can attach them to their barrette.

- The shape will serve as the cherry on top of participants' creations because it is the piece they have spent the most time developing. Encourage them to layer it in front of other materials—for example, as the centerpiece of a fabric bow, on top of a foam cutout heart, or jauntily glued on top of a more simple shape that has been painted with paint pens.
- Participants should feel free to use the paint pens on their shape to give it some dimension.
- Give participants time to admire each other's creations and take inspiration from each other! Explain how small fashion brands use 3-D printing to allow designers, such as your participants, to develop their brands and reproduce wearable art. If 3-D print services are available in your library, now is the perfect time to encourage participants to take advantage of their new skills by offering free print time or further structured assistance.

LEARNING OUTCOMES

Participants will . . .
- Understand the basic mechanics of the 3-D printer.
- Grasp the basic functions of 3-D modeling software, including additive and subtractive modeling and the z-axis.
- Learn about 3-D printing's application in small business manufacturing and begin to develop branded designs of their own.

RECOMMENDED NEXT PROJECTS

This project is a great introduction to 3-D modeling and printing, so participants are more than ready to tackle more advanced 3-D printing projects. Those who enjoyed making multiples and the potential for trading and collecting may enjoy projects from part 6, Vinyl Cutting and Sticker Projects, in this book.

3-D Printed Animal Earrings

SARA RUSSELL GONZALEZ
Science Librarian, Marston Science Library, University of Florida

JEAN L. BOSSART
Engineering Librarian, Marston Science Library, University of Florida

FANG-YI (TIFFANY) SU
Graduate Student in Fine Arts, University of Florida

MAKING ANIMAL EARRINGS is a fun way to explore 3-D printing. Patrons will learn how to find a 3-D model of an animal on the free open-source repository Thingiverse.com and use another free program, Tinkercad .com, to resize the model and modify the animal to add a loop for the earring wire. Whether it's a farm animal, exotic animal, or pet, making 3-D printed animal jewelry is a great way to learn about 3-D printing.

Age Range	Type of Library Best Suited For	Cost Estimate
Tweens (ages 8–12) Young adults (ages 13–18) Adults	Public libraries Academic libraries School libraries	$20–$30

OVERVIEW

This is a great project for a workshop where participants want to model and 3-D print a small object in one session. Typically, this isn't doable because

3-D printing is a slow process; however, these tiny animals turned into earrings are very fast to print (about 3 minutes) and patrons should be able to leave with a finished set they created themselves.

The number of participants will be determined by your number of computers and 3-D printers. We recommend starting with a short introduction to 3-D printing and Thingiverse, followed by a guided tour of Tinkercad. You may wish to provide step-by-step guidance on resizing and adding the loop to the animals or give them written instructions to follow at their own pace.

For younger children, you may wish to skip Thingiverse and Tinkercad and just focus on painting and adding the wire to make earrings. We have been surprised, however, at how quickly children learn Tinkercad, especially those who already have experience

Figure 26.1 | Three finished pairs of earrings using the French hook ball dot ear wires

with Minecraft. We recommend that you have models already printed and also print during the workshop so they can see the finished product and the technology in action.

Materials List

- 3-D filament (we recommend PLA)
- Earring hooks, such as French hook ball dot ear wires

Optional Materials
- Paint
  - *Hint:* Nail polish works well on small plastic models.
- Small paintbrush
- Sharpies
- 20- to 22- gauge wire
- Seed beads

Necessary Equipment

- Computer with Internet access
- 3-D printer
- Small needle-nose pliers

STEP-BY-STEP INSTRUCTIONS

Project Instructions

CHOOSE AN ANIMAL

Find a model from an online repository, such as Thingiverse.com.

- Search for your favorite animal.
- To have a better chance of a successful 3-D print, only select animals that have been printed by other users. Look for actual photos rather than computer-generated images.
- Avoid models with very fine features because you will be printing them in miniature and that detail will probably be lost. Models that use basic shapes to depict the animal will be the most successful.
- Download the .stl 3-D file.
- Recommended models to try
  - Elephant: www.thingiverse.com/thing:2803935
  - Pig: www.thingiverse.com/thing:3119221
  - Sheep: www.thingiverse.com/thing:2387435
  - Stackable sheep: www.thingiverse.com/thing:474526
  - Polar bear: www.thingiverse.com/thing:1200701
  - Whale: www.thingiverse.com/thing:767237

ADD LOOP IN TINKERCAD

Most models will not have a hole to insert the ear wire so we recommend using Tinkercad to add a loop.

- Log on to Tinkercad.com and create a new account if you have never used it before. Patrons younger than 13 years old will need a parent to approve the account. Tinkercad offers online tutorials for new users that we recommend you complete first if this is your first time using 3-D modeling software.
- Import the .stl file
- Click on the model and hold down Shift while dragging the white box that changes the model's height until it is around 20 millimeters. Using Shift will scale the animal proportionally.

- Pull over a tube icon from the side menu.
- Rotate tube 90 degrees and change size of loop to 2 millimeters. Be sure to scale proportionally.
- Move loop to top of animal and overlap it with the animal just enough that the loop is securely embedded in the animal's body. Make sure that enough of the loop is outside the animal so that you can fit the wire through the loop.
- Export the animal and loop as an .stl file.

3-D PRINT THE ANIMAL

- Import the 3-D file you just created in Tinkercad into your 3-D printer software (example: Cura, Simplify3D).
- Duplicate the model so that you have two animals for the earrings.
- Set the 3-D printing parameters. We recommend a layer thickness of 0.15 to 0.20 millimeters and to try it first without support. Many models will be small enough that support is not necessary. Also, leave off a raft unless the model will not stay attached to the build plate.
- Any plastic filament is fine to use, although we recommend PLA. You may wish to choose a color that matches the animal (such as pink for a pig), but remember that you can also paint the model afterward.

ADD EARRING WIRES TO ANIMAL

- There are several different types of ear wires that you can use. If you have a small loop, you can use a French hook ball dot ear wire that simply slides through the loop. The earring is then ready to wear.

Figure 26.2 | The left image shows the scaled animal model and the tube shape rotated. The right image is after the tube is scaled to a height of 5 millimeters and overlapping the top of the animal.

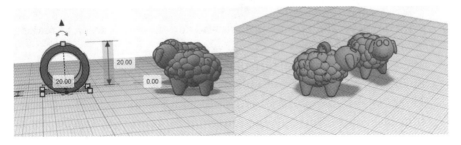

- Another option is to use a fish earring hook that has a loop at the end. You will then use your needle-nose pliers to gently open up the wire loop, slip it through the animal loop, and then close it tightly. Make sure that the wire loop is closed fully, or otherwise, the animal may slip off.
- If you wish to make the earrings more dangly, try using 20- to 22-gauge wire. Using the needle-nose pliers, make a loop at the end of the wire and attach it to the animal model. Add seed beads above the animal and then make another loop. Attach this to the earring wire for a complete earring.

ADDITIONAL ACTIVITIES (OPTIONAL)

If time permits, you may wish to paint your animal. Acrylic paint works well on models printed with PLA and is inexpensive at hobby stores.

- Use a small paintbrush to dab on paint. The models are tiny, so this is very fine detailed work, and children may be discouraged if their model is ruined. Use scrap plastic to practice painting before attempting the real model. You may wish to print out multiples of animals because the 3-D prints are typically extremely fast.
- In lieu of paint, try using Sharpie markers to color the models.

LEARNING OUTCOMES

Participants will . . .

- Learn how to find printable 3-D models using the Thingiverse.com repository.
- Develop 3-D modeling skills using Tinkercad.com.
- Learn how to use pliers and attach ear wires to make earrings.

RECOMMENDED NEXT PROJECTS

- Print out several different animals and add them to a chain to make a charm bracelet.
- Make larger animals and turn them into a necklace.
- Build additional expertise in Tinkercad and create new models of animals. These can then be uploaded and shared with other users in Thingiverse. com. Make sure to introduce patrons to the concept of Creative Commons licensing.

Kawaii 3-D Prints for Back to School

JAMIE BAIR

Senior Public Services Librarian: Experiential Learning,
Fort Vancouver Regional Libraries

PARTICIPANTS WILL USE Tinkercad to create super cute creations that can be modified to add to pencils, books, bags, and more. Using basic shapes and general kawaii aesthetics, participants can create truly individual designs.

Age Range	Type of Library Best Suited For
Tweens (ages 8–12)	Public libraries
Young adults (ages 13–18)	Academic libraries
Adults	School libraries

Cost Estimate

- $0–$20
- This project is low to no-cost. Tinkercad is a free, cloud-based 3-D modeling platform. This project is crafted on the assumption that participants have access to a 3-D printer to print completed models. Filament cost to print these objects is negligible.

OVERVIEW

This project has an easy and a challenge mode. If participants are new to 3-D modeling, they can gain experience working with Tinkercad by remixing the

premodeled kawaii template. Older participants
or those who need more
of a challenge will learn
the basic concepts of
modeling kawaii objects
in Tinkercad to create
their own designs!

Figure 27.1 | Kawaii bookmark, paperclip, and keychain

Materials List

Optional Materials

- Download the
  Kawaii STL files
  and detailed
  instructions from
  Dropbox: http://bit.ly/kawaiib2s
- Acrylic paint and brushes to customize prints
- Hot glue to attach face to pencil topper

Necessary Equipment

- 3-D printer (if printing final objects)
- Computer with Internet access

STEP-BY-STEP INSTRUCTIONS

Preparation

- Project facilitators should sign up for a Tinkercad account before the
  workshop. Familiarize yourself with the basic modeling components:
  changing shapes into solids/holes, aligning objects, rotating views, resizing using the ruler, undo/redo, and grouping and ungrouping objects.
  The Tinkercad community has created a lot of great tutorials around
  these key skills.
- Project facilitators should locate the updated kawaii template on Tinkercad. Search Tinkercad for "bluebair" under "people" and "kawaii
  template" under "3-D design."

- The kawaii template includes the following:
  - » Four bases: pencil topper, heart bookmark, rectangle paperclip, keychain loop
  - » Three mouths (solid) + one mouth (hole)
  - » Two eye sets (solid) + one eye set (hole)
  - » Two ear sets (solid)
  - » One face template
  - » Three completed face examples
- Click on the project to open a preview and then click the "Copy and Tinker" button.
- You can also access individual .stl files of each piece and detailed instructions in Dropbox: http://bit.ly/kawaiib2s.
- Participants are encouraged to sign up for a Tinkercad account. Individual accounts encourage users to return to their models to continue developing their 3-D modeling skills.

PROJECT INSTRUCTIONS

Beginner and complex projects will both follow the same kawaii design principles:

- Facial features are oversized.
- Facial features are aligned close to the center of the face.

Tips for Tinkercad

- You can undo up to 20 mistakes. Don't get too far along in your project!
- The Ruler tool (upper right-hand side) lets you make precise measurement changes quickly. It can be dragged onto the workplane and dismissed as often as needed.
- The arrow keys on a standard computer keyboard can be used to make fine placement adjustments of objects. The Snap Grid (lower right-hand side) can be changed to make larger or smaller adjustments.
- The shape modifier window allows you to change the colors of your objects as well as change the shapes into solids or holes. To make a completely round cylinder, try adjusting the Sides slider to 64.
- You must group a hole with a solid object before you can see the piece carved out.

- Shapes floating above or below the workplane can be quickly reset by clicking on the object and selecting the "D" key on the keyboard.

Beginner: Remixing Models

- Participants should locate the kawaii template on Tinkercad. Instructions on locating the file are listed in the Preparation section of this project.
- Participants will copy template pieces into a new project.
    - Locate the copy of the kawaii template and click the "Tinker this" button.
    - Click on the blank face template (oval in the bottom left of workplane) and Ctrl + C to create a copy.
    - Return to the main designs screen and click "Create new design."
    - Ctrl + V to paste the face template onto the blank workplane.
    - Repeat these steps to copy other template pieces to a new project.
        » Eyes and ears are grouped as one piece to maintain correct spacing.
        » Grouped objects can be ungrouped by selecting the items and clicking "Ungroup" or Ctrl + Shift + G.
        » Click off the objects to choose individual pieces.
    - Once all pieces have been copied to the new project, close the template for later use.
- Working in the new design, participants start remixing the object by choosing a nose and/or mouth to add to the blank face template.
    - Click and drag a box around the face and nose/mouth or Shift + click on both objects.
    - Choose "Align" tool in upper-right.
    - Align nose in the center of the face.
    - Repeat these steps to set the eyes. Eyes should be aligned with the nose.
    - Use the keyboard arrows to make fine adjustments to feature placement. Change Snap Grid (lower right) to make smaller adjustments.
    - Align ears to top of face.
    - Check placement by selecting all objects and grouping to see final object. Ungroup the objects to adjust features.
    - Experiment with turning objects into holes or holes in solid objects. Regroup the features and note how this changes the face.

- When participants are ready to export their completed 3-D object, do the following:
  - Group the final features together to create one object.
  - Click on grouped object, and then choose "Export."
  - In the download menu, include "the selected shape."
  - Choose .stl to download the 3-D model.
  - The model is now ready to load into 3-D printer slicing software for slicing and printing.

Complex: Design Your Own

- Participants should click "Create new design" from the main Tinkercad screen.
- Participants are encouraged to try different shapes, sizes, and arrangements. The example provided in this section is a jumping-off point, not a finished product.

Face Base
- Participants choose a base shape for their object from the basic shapes menu on the right side. Cylinders, boxes, hearts, and stars are all easy base shapes to manipulate.
- Drag out the ruler to resize the object.
  - Know the minimum layer height for your 3-D printer (generally 1 millimeter).
  - Resize the base shape to create a flat work surface. The example is sized: x = 40 millimeters, y = 30 millimeters, and z = 4 millimeters.
  - Flat objects or objects with a wide flat base are recommended for first-time printers.

Eyes
- Experiment with different shapes to make eyes.
  - Example eyes instructions (based on face x = 40 millimeters, y = 30 millimeters, and z = 4 millimeters) include the following:
    » Cylinder x = 9.5 millimeters, y =11 millimeters, z = 7 millimeters.
    » Duplicate cylinder, resize duplicate x = 4 millimeters, y = 4 millimeters, z = 7 millimeters.
    » Align cylinders along right edge.
    » Use keyboard keys to shift smaller cylinder slightly down.

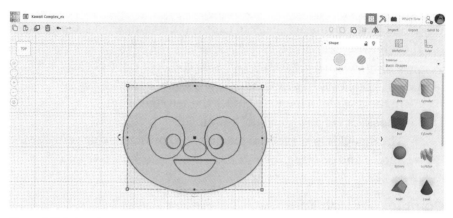

Figure 27.2 | Complex example

> » Change smaller cylinder to hole.
> » Group both cylinders into eye.
> » Duplicate eye. Flip along x-axis.
> » Use keyboard arrows to adjust placement.
> » Select both eyes and align centered on the x-axis.
> – Z = 7 millimeters to ensure the object sits on top of the face 3 millimeters (face is 4 millimeters). Experiment with creating taller and shorter eyes. Inset the eyes by creating holes and grouping with face.

Nose

- Experiment with different shapes to make a nose.
  - Example nose instructions (based on face x = 40 millimeters, y = 30 millimeters, z = 4 millimeters) include the following:
    - » Cylinder x = 6 millimeters, y = 4 millimeters, z = 7 millimeters.

Mouth

- Experiment with different shapes to make a mouth.
  - Example mouth instructions (based on face x = 40 millimeters, y = 30 millimeters, z = 4 millimeters) include the following:
    - » Cylinder x = 20 millimeters, y = 20 millimeters, z = 7 millimeters.
    - » Box hole. Align to cover upper side of cylinder. Group objects.

Putting It All Together
- Align eyes, nose, mouth, and face centered.
- Use keyboard arrows to make fine adjustments.
- Resize objects to avoid overlap.
- Group shapes.
- From here, add more embellishments: Ears? Top hat? Eyelashes?
- When participants are ready to export their completed 3-D object,
    - Group the final features together to create one object.
    - Click on grouped object, and then choose "Export."
    - In the download menu, include "the selected shape."
    - Choose .stl to download the 3-D model.
    - The model is now ready to load into 3-D printer slicing software for slicing and printing.

LEARNING OUTCOMES

Participants will . . .
- Practice using basic 3-D modeling software.
- Manipulate objects to create unique designs.
- Prepare 3-D models for printing.

RECOMMENDED NEXT PROJECTS

- Chapter 26: 3-D Printed Animal Earrings
- Chapter 28: 3-D Printed Kawaii Cat Keychain

3-D Printed Kawaii Cat Keychain

PHILLIP BALLO
Library Assistant, Southwestern Community College District

IN THIS PROJECT, you will learn how to make a simple 3-D printed keychain. When designing a cat, imagine either just a flat 2-D design or a full 3-D design. The 2-D design is less complicated and uses less filament, but the 3-D method can be adapted to create toys and more complicated designs. This project is best for makerspace professionals who have experience 3-D modeling and 3-D printing and best for libraries with free access laboratories.

Age Range
Tweens (ages 8–12)
Young adults (ages 13–18)
Adults

Type of Library Best Suited For
Public libraries
Academic libraries
School libraries

Cost Estimate

- $1–$50
- The initial investment includes a 3-D printing reel, clasps, and key rings. If you buy in bulk, each keychain should cost around $1.
- This project assumes that you already own the tools, including the 3-D printer and does not include the electrical costs.

Figure 28.1 | 3-D models printed out

OVERVIEW

I occasionally do 3-D modeling as part of my hobby, and when 3-D printing came around, it was an easy transition. This project is best for students who have some experience with 3-D modeling, but anyone should be able to do this project.

This project should be divided into three parts: sketching and planning, 3-D modeling, and 3-D printing. Sketching and the 3-D modeling part should take maybe more than an hour if you keep it simple by using only primitive shapes and Boolean modifiers. Be aware that 3-D printing an object may take a long time, so be sure to account for this time. Additionally, depending on experience and possibly age group, teaching 3-D modeling may take a couple of sessions, especially if students need to resculpt or repair the model later on. If you are pressed for time, using a 3-D relief model would be easier and would still help students translate 2-D sketch images into 3-D models. Additionally, the 3-D relief model has a higher chance of success with 3-D printing. The number of participants should be limited to the amount of 3-D printers available. Due to the potential variances of 3-D models by your students, you may not be able to provide everyone a 3-D printed model, unless students are allowed to access 3-D printers outside of the class.

Materials List

- Lobster clasp or a key ring
- Several jump rings
- Filament

Optional Materials

- Permanent marker
- Sealant
- Paint
- Sandpaper
- Paper clips, twine, wires, or zip ties (as an alternative to buying a keychain)

These materials are meant for finishing your project. The permanent marker is meant to draw on the face of the cat if your 3-D printer is unable to capture the details properly.

Necessary Equipment

- 3-D printer
- Two pliers (for bending the jump rings)

STEP-BY-STEP INSTRUCTIONS

Preparation

Is your cat fully 3-D or do you want your cat to be flat with a 3-D relief texture? A 3-D relief texture is less likely to fail while printing and uses less material overall.

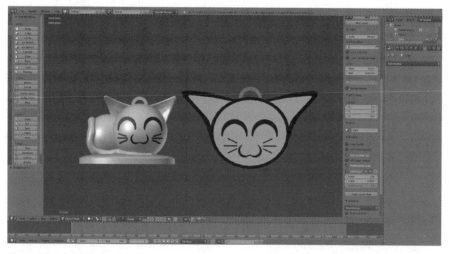

Figure 28.2 | A 3-D model of a cat on a pillow and a simple 3-D cat relief print; modeled in Blender

PROJECT INSTRUCTIONS

- Sketch out your cat. Try to imagine how the 3-D printer will print out the object, particularly if there are complicated shapes, creases, and overhangs.
- 3-D model your cat using your favorite 3-D modeling program. For beginners, try to avoid sculpting and use only primitive shapes. If you combine shapes using destructive modifiers (such as Boolean modifiers), be sure to save a copy of each shape or a copy of the project to ensure that you are able to fix the object after 3-D printing.
- Check for and repair any intersecting faces, interior faces, or broken faces.
- Export your 3-D model as a 3-D printer slicer compatible file such as an .stl file.
- Repair your model using your slicer's 3-D repair program or an online service.
- Preview your file and see if there are any potential 3-D printing complications, such as broken faces, steep overhangs, and so on.
- Add the necessary 3-D print supports.
- 3-D print your object.
- If your 3-D print did not print out correctly, try adjusting the size or adjust the shapes of your model.
- Once you 3-D print your model, add your finishing touches, such as painting it or polishing it. If there are any sharp corners, sand them down or remodel your 3-D model. If you just want to keep it as it is, skip this step.
- Take a key ring or a lobster clasp and add jump rings to the appropriate location using your two pliers. Add enough jump rings to your desired length.
- Attach the final jump ring to the cat and chain.

LEARNING OUTCOMES

Participants will . . .
- Learn how to plan a 3-D modeling project from sketch to physical object.
- Learn the basics of 3-D modeling.
- Learn how 3-D printing works.
- Learn how to repair 3-D models for 3-D printing.

RECOMMENDED NEXT PROJECTS

3-D modeling is probably the hardest part of this project. However, once participants get the gist of 3-D modeling, they can move on to learn precise 3-D modeling using exact measurements, which will allow them to incorporate electronics into their projects.

3-D Printed Succulent Pot

NATALIE SPAAN

Youth Services Coordinator, Caledon Public Library

AT CALEDON PUBLIC Library, our 3-D printer is rarely left unused! Between class visits and in-house programming, the constant buzz and hum of our MakerBot have just become part of our daily work life. Although we always encourage patrons to be creative and come up with their own designs in our 3-D printing sessions, we often find that having prototypes on hand can help to spark their own imagination. These simple succulent pots are one such example. Starting with a basic design, tweens can then decorate their pots in whatever artistic way they see fit, from adding simple kawaii faces, to turning them into adorable animals, to even adapting them to look like their favorite Pokémon!

Age Range	Type of Library Best Suited For
Tweens (ages 8–12)	Public libraries School libraries

Cost Estimate

- $0
- Cost is dependent on the price of the filament used in your specific 3-D printer and on whether you decide to supply succulent plants.

OVERVIEW

When it comes to 3-D design, we have found that Tinkercad is the easiest software to use in programming, especially for beginners. The fact that it is web-based and free to use is a great bonus! There are also several quick and easy step-by-step tutorials online to help introduce Tinkercad to those who haven't used it before. When running 3-D design classes, we generally log participants into our library's Tinkercad account to make it easy for staff to access the models and print them at a later date.

Because the pots themselves are quite simple to create, minimal staff assistance is required, and your program size is only limited

Figure 29.1 | A completed pot with an added succulent!

by the number of computers your participants have access to. Depending on the skill and experience of those attending, the pots could take anywhere from 20 minutes to an hour to design and complete. Our regular attendees with greater skill using Tinkercad tend to use their extra time experimenting with ways to make their designs better or come up with something completely different!

Due to the fact that these pots will need to be printed at a later time, you could potentially plan this to be a two-day program and invite participants back the following week to paint their designs and plant succulents too!

Materials List

- 3-D printer filament

Optional Materials
- Paint
- Succulents
- Dirt
- Moss

Necessary Equipment

- 3-D printer
- Computers/laptops
- Internet access

STEP-BY-STEP INSTRUCTIONS

Preparation

- Create a Tinkercad account for your library at www.tinkercad.com.
- Practice creating and printing a pot beforehand to better assist participants who are having issues with the design.

PROJECT INSTRUCTIONS

- Log participants into Tinkercad using your library's account.
- Allow first-time users to try some of Tinkercad's quick tutorials to get a handle on the various tools that they can use in the program.

Making the Basic Pot

- Those who are comfortable using Tinkercad can begin by selecting a sphere and placing it on the workplane.
- Enlarge the sphere until it is a good size to hold a small plant. A circumference of roughly 130 millimeters is a good place to start, as the size of the planter can be tweaked again when downloaded to your 3-D printer.
- Select a cylinder and place it inside the sphere. Enlarge the cylinder and click on the Hole option under the dropdown Shape menu. This will create the hole for your plant to sit in. Make sure to raise the cylinder up using the black triangle on top of the shape, otherwise your hole will go straight through the entire pot. You can check to make sure that your hole is positioned correctly by selecting both the sphere and the cylinder (press and hold Shift while clicking both shapes) and group them together (Ctrl + G).
- Participants can now decorate their pot however they wish!

Adding a Kawaii Face

- An easy way to make these pots cute is to draw on a kawaii face using the Scribble tool. Start by clicking and dragging a new workplane to the front of your pot.
- Find the Scribble shape and click and drag it to the spot where you would like the face to go. This will open up a new design screen for you to draw the face.
- Use the pencil tool to draw your desired kawaii face. Looking at examples of different faces from the Internet might help! Once you are happy with your design, you can click the Done button in the bottom right-hand corner.
- To imprint the face into the pot, select the hole button and push the face partially into the pot.

Saving the Pot

- Select and group all the objects in Tinkercad together (Ctrl + G).
- Save the Tinkercad file by changing the name in the top left-hand corner to the first name and last initial of the participant.
- The pot can now be downloaded and printed as an .stl file to your 3-D printer!

LEARNING OUTCOMES

Participants will . . .
- Understand how 3-D printers work.
- Learn to place and manipulate shapes using basic 3-D design software.
- Discover how easy it is to create their own everyday objects.

RECOMMENDED NEXT PROJECTS

- Chapter 25: Decora Hair Barrettes
- Chapter 28: 3-D Printed Kawaii Cat Keychain
- 3-D Printed Cookie Cutters

PART V

JEWELRY PROJECTS

Button Making

CHANTALE PARD
Youth Services Librarian, Keshen Goodman Public Library

BUTTON MAKING IS an exciting activity for people of all ages—everyone loves to represent their favorite fandom or style with this cute little accessory. People wear buttons on their shirts, pin them to their book bags, clip them to their convention lanyards, or even tack them to a bulletin board. Creators can choose from a variety of different designs by DIYing their own piece or cutting out their favorite image from the predesigned selections from library staff.

Age Range	Type of Library Best Suited For
Kids (ages 3–7) Tweens (ages 8–12) Young adults (ages 13–18) Adults	Public libraries Academic libraries School libraries

Cost Estimate

- $300 (includes purchase of a button maker machine)
- **Cost note:** Although the initial cost for this project might seem quite steep, buying the consumable button parts in bulk should allow you to rerun the program many more times at zero cost because you'll already have the button maker machine.

OVERVIEW

It's unlikely that this project will occupy program attendees for a full hour—but it might take staff the entire 60 minutes to oversee the button pressing for each creator if the program is well attended. Button making works well as an activity station—perhaps a day-long drop-in table at an academic or school library—or as a single activity station in a larger, themed program that also has more staff.

The smaller size (1¼ inches) of these buttons means they are fairly cute as is, regardless of the carried image, but creators can amp up the kawaii by putting traditionally adorable items inside—think magical girls, baby animals, anthropomorphized food, or stationery.

Materials List

- 1¼-inch button pieces
  - Can be purchased from Tecre.com or PeoplePowerPress.net. Try the following:
    » Everything for Lock-Pin Buttons: These are cheaper because they require an extra assembly step.

Figure 30.1 | Kawaii buttons displaying digital art from anime club teens

» Everything for Pinback Buttons: These have one less assembly step but are a bit more expensive than the lock-pin version.
- Printed 1¼-inch button circle templates filled with copyright-free kawaii images
- Printed 1¼-inch blank button circle templates for decorating freehand
- Color pencils or markers

Necessary Equipment
- Tecre 125 (1¼-inch) Round Button Making Machine
  - Can be purchased from Tecre.com.
- Scissors

STEP-BY-STEP INSTRUCTIONS

Preparation

- Save a variety of copyright-free kawaii images to your computer.
- You can print off 1¼-inch button circle templates filled with copyright-free kawaii images.
  - Google "free 1¼-inch button template" and save your chosen template image.
  - To create a fillable circle template, insert the saved template image into a Microsoft Publisher document.
  - Click on Insert > Shapes and then click on the circle.
  - Draw circles on top of each *inner* circle shape, using the template as your size guide.
    » Remember to keep the *outer halo* circle free of images, as this is the space that is meant to wrap around the button back.
    » Overhang is fine in the halo as long as the creator realizes it won't be visible on the finished button.
  - To fill each circle with a different picture, click on the circle > Format > Fill Effects > Picture > Select Picture, then browse through your folders to find your previously saved kawaii images for insertion.
- Or you can even make your own kawaii images on Canva.com.
  - Make a free account with your e-mail address.
  - Click "Create a Design," then "Custom Dimensions."
  - Input 8.5 × 11 inches, then click "Create new design."

- Select "Uploads" from the left-side menu and upload your free 1¼-inch button template as a picture into the document.
- Search for "kawaii," "cute," "kittens," "unicorns," "fruit," and so on in the left-side search bar. Select "Graphics" to narrow down your search to transparent items that will fit in the circle ("Photos" could work too if you're ready to play with the sizing).
- When you've finished all your circle designs, click the download button in the top right corner (the down arrow), save the file as a .jpg, and then color print it.
- Alternatively, if you purchase or obtain the free trial of "Canva for Work" (which gives you free access to all the crown images), you will have wider access to kawaii pictures in addition to the kawaii face transparencies, which you can insert over any inanimate object to make them look instantly adorable.
- If you go the free trial route, make sure to download as many kawaii images as you can while you have access—this way you'll have a back stock for the next time you run the program, instead of having to pay for access.
  » That said, Canva really is an excellent, intuitive poster-making site, and the upgraded account has worked well for us at Keshen Goodman Public Library, so it's worth the money, if you have it, in my opinion.
- Print off blank versions of that same 1¼-inch button template for decorating freehand with art supplies.
- Library staff should watch Tecre's YouTube instructional video for how to use the button machine before making any buttons. The instructions are quite simple and easy to remember once you get the hang of it, but placing the button pieces in the wrong die, or at the wrong time, can jam the expensive machine.

Project Instructions

- Creators arrive and decide if they want to create their own image in a blank circle template, or if they'd like to cut out a preprinted circle image.
- Remind creators that they are decorating only the inner circle of the blank templates, but when cutting their button images (hand-drawn or computer printed), they need to cut carefully along the outer circle line.

- Once creators have cut their circles, they can approach staff to use the button machine.
- Staff should set the button pieces in the machine according to the proper method, explaining verbal instructions to the creator as they do.
- Once the pieces are in the correct places, staff should invite the creator to pull the

Figure 30.2 | Buttons made out of manga and comic book discards for free comic book day prizes

lever down in order to press the button (some younger children will be too weak to do this, though—I would only offer the lever pull portion of the process to children who seem strong enough).
- Once both sides of the button have been pressed, the button will be ready to go!

LEARNING OUTCOMES

Participants will . . .
- Learn how to use tools like the button-making machine.
- Use their art skills by drawing unique kawaii designs.
- Express their unique creativity and fandoms through button creation.

RECOMMENDED NEXT PROJECTS

- In addition to button pieces, try purchasing magnet backs and zipper pulls, which also work with the Tecre button machine.
- Discarded comic book, novel, or manga pages can also work as great images to make into buttons too.
- Don't forget: buttons are also a quick and easy low-cost prize option for many other library programs! Whip up a cute little set of matching buttons, attach them to a piece of cardstock labeled in glittery gel pen, and you have an exciting, no-cost giveaway for your next trivia program or poetry contest.

31

Bottle Cap Jewelry

CHANTALE PARD
Youth Services Librarian, Keshen Goodman Public Library

BOTTLE CAP JEWELRY provides a variety of options to create adorable accessories—from necklaces to key chains, to magnets, and so on. Creators can design their own chibi art or decorate with a variety of cute stickers to show off their kawaii style.

Age Range	Type of Library Best Suited For
Tweens (ages 8-12) Young adults (ages 13-18)	Public libraries School libraries

Cost Estimate

- $40–$50
- **Cost note:** Although the initial cost for this project might seem a bit steep, buying consumable supplies in bulk (such as the bottle caps, epoxy dots, and jump rings) should allow you to rerun the program a few more times at zero cost because you'll already have the metal hole punch tool.

OVERVIEW

Depending on the amount of customization or number of pieces being made, this activity might not take the full time of a one-hour program slot. I usually run it as a supplemental activity alongside other themed projects over the course of the hour, or even as the single craft option during anime club, while we watch our episode of the month.

Older teens might be comfortable using the jump rings, pliers, and hot glue gun themselves, whereas you'll want to keep this equipment under strict staff supervision when working with younger youth.

Materials List

- Bottle caps
  - These can be purchased in bulk craft stores or on Amazon.com in a variety of colors—make sure you're getting the linerless, craft variety.
- 1-inch clear epoxy dots
  - These can be purchased in bulk craft stores or on Amazon.com.
  - You'll need one for each bottle cap you're planning to use during the program.
  - These provide a resin-like look and finish to the project without having to fiddle with any resin chemicals.
- Glitter

Figure 31.1 | Kawaii bottle cap necklaces

- Smaller kawaii stickers
  - Items that will fit within the 1-inch circle
  - They must be thin/flat
- Printed 1-inch bottle cap circle templates filled with copyright-free kawaii images
- Printed blank 1-inch bottle cap circle templates for decorating freehand
- Color pencils
- Markers
- Embroidery thread, thin elastic, or anything to make necklaces

Optional Supplies
- Jump rings
- Mini magnets
- Key rings

Necessary Equipment
- Scissors
- Hot glue gun
- Metal bottle cap hole punch
  - Try EuroTools or BCI Crafts brand—found on Amazon.com or in craft stores.

Optional Supplies
- Bent ring pliers
  - Try purchasing a jump ring kit that includes a variety of jump rings, bent nose pliers, and a ring opener tool. These can be found online for around $20.

STEP-BY-STEP INSTRUCTIONS

Preparation

- Buy a variety of kawaii stickers that will fit within the 1-inch circle space.
- Save a variety of copyright-free kawaii images to your computer.
- You can print off 1-inch bottle cap circle templates filled with copyright-free kawaii images.
  - Google "free 1-inch circle template" and save your chosen template image.

- To create a fillable circle template, insert the saved template image in Microsoft Publisher.
- Click on Insert > Shapes and then click on the circle.
- Draw circles on top of each template circle shape, using the inserted template picture as your size guide.
- To fill each circle with a different picture, click on the circle > Format > Fill Effects > Picture > Select Picture, then browse through your folders to find your previously saved kawaii images for insertion.

Figure 31.2 | Bottle cap jewelry supplies

- Print off blank versions of that same 1-inch bottle cap circle templates for decorating freehand with art supplies.
- Or you can even make your own kawaii images on Canva.com.
  - Make a free account with your e-mail address.
  - Click "Create a Design," then "Custom Dimensions."
  - Input 100 × 100 pixels, then click "Create new design."
  - Select "Elements" from the left side menu, and click on "Circle" under "Shapes."
  - Use your mouse on the corner of the inserted circle to drag the size to "w:96 h:96," which means 96 pixels and also means it will print as a 1-inch circle.
  - You can then adjust the background color or transparency of the circle.
  - Search for "kawaii," "cute," "kittens," "unicorns," "fruit," and so on in the left-side search bar. Select "Graphics" to narrow down your search to transparent items that will fit in the circle ("Photos" could work too if you're ready to play with the sizing).
  - When you've finished your 1-inch circle design, click the download button in the top right corner (the down arrow), and save the file as a .jpg. You can then insert the circle multiple times over into a Microsoft Word or Publisher document, or continue to make different circle designs in Canva. I recommend putting a lot of circles onto one main page in Publisher so that you're not wasting paper.

- Alternatively, if you purchase or obtain the free trial of "Canva for Work" (which gives you free access to all the crown images), you will have wider access to kawaii pictures—in addition to the kawaii face transparencies, which you can insert over any inanimate object to make it look instantly adorable.
- If you go the free trial route, make sure to download as many kawaii images as you can while you have access—this way you'll have a back stock for the next time you run the program, instead of having to pay for "Canva for Work" access again.
- That said, Canva really is an excellent, intuitive poster-making site, and the upgraded account has worked well for us at Keshen Goodman Public Library.

PROJECT INSTRUCTIONS

- Creators arrive and select their bottle caps.
- They can then decide if they want to create their own image in a blank circle template, if they'd like to cut out a preprinted circle image, or if they want to fill the space with the provided stickers.
- Remind creators that they are decorating the underneath/inside of the bottle cap.
- Once creators have cut out their 1-inch circle designs (hand-drawn or computer printed), they will need to be hot glued to the bottle caps (have staff complete this portion for younger children).
  - Apply hot glue to the bottle cap in a quick, swirly motion, taking care not to create a large uneven lump, before carefully pressing paper circle to it.
  - If using stickers only, hot glue shouldn't be necessary.
- Creators can now carefully place a glitter layer if they desire—larger flat glitter pieces work best and should ideally be glued down (a tiny dab of white glue can work for this instead of a hot glue bead).
  - **Please note:** If glitter is left unglued, the epoxy dot from the next step won't stick to the circle image. It might be possible to get by without gluing if the glitter used is very fine and sparing, but it's better to be safe and not waste the dot if it doesn't end up sticking.
- Carefully place a clear epoxy dot on top of bottle cap design.
  - No glue needed here—the dot is sticky enough. Glue will only create a foggy coating on top of the design, making it less visible.

- Try not to touch the sticky bottom of the epoxy, as fingerprints can also be visible through the sticker.
- It's now time to punch the hole in the bottle cap with the tool. Take care to have it right in the top-middle of the wavy outer edge.
  - **Pro tip:** for jump-ring-less necklaces, bracelets, and so on, create two side-by-side hole punches in the top center to create a centered thread loop.
- If using jump rings, use pliers and ring tool kits to insert the jump ring into punched hole before adding it to a key ring or necklace string.
- Alternatively, avoid the hole punch, and hot glue a small magnet piece to the back of the bottle cap creation.

LEARNING OUTCOMES

Participants will . . .
- Learn how to use jewelry-making tools such as the metal hole punch and pliers.
- Use their art skills by drawing unique kawaii designs.
- Express their creativity through jewelry creation.

RECOMMENDED NEXT PROJECTS

- If you have leftover supplies from your new bottle cap jewelry-making kit, chapter 32, Kawaii Holiday Ornaments, should be super simple!
- For more kawaii jewelry projects, check out chapter 34, Bubble Pendants, and chapter 37, Laser-Cut Steampunk Gear Jewelry.

32

Kawaii Holiday Ornaments

CHANTALE PARD

Youth Services Librarian, Keshen Goodman Public Library

KAWAII HOLIDAY ORNAMENTS take the basics of bottle cap jewelry making to provide a festive cute spin on Christmas tree baubles. Creators can design their own chibi holiday art or decorate with a variety of cute stickers or printouts. Completed crafts can be hung on their family trees, given as holiday gifts, or used in any way they may see fit to celebrate the chilly season.

Age Range	Type of Library Best Suited For
Tweens (ages 8–12) Young adults (ages 13–18)	Public libraries

Cost Estimate

- $30–$40
- **Cost note:** Although the initial cost for this project might seem a bit steep, buying consumable supplies in bulk (such as the bottle caps, epoxy dots, and jump rings) should allow you to rerun the program a few more times at zero cost because you'll already have the metal hole punch tool.

OVERVIEW

Depending on the amount of customization or number of pieces being made, this activity might not take the full time of a one-hour program slot. I usually run it as a supplemental activity alongside other holiday projects over the course of the hour. Try including a simple festive hot chocolate station to round out the event.

Figure 32.1 | Kawaii holiday ornaments made by teens in our anime club

Materials List

- Bottle caps
  - These can be purchased in bulk craft stores or on Amazon.com in a variety of colors—make sure you're getting the linerless, craft variety.
- 1-inch clear epoxy dots
  - These can be purchased in bulk craft stores or on Amazon.com.
  - You'll need one for each bottle cap you're planning to use during the program.
  - These provide a resin-like look and finish to the project without having to fiddle with any resin chemicals.
- Glitter
- Smaller kawaii stickers
  - Items must fit within the 1-inch circle.
  - These must be thin/flat.
- Printed 1-inch bottle cap circle templates filled with copyright-free kawaii holiday images
- Printed blank 1-inch bottle cap circle templates for decorating freehand
- Color pencils
- Markers
- Embroidery thread, elastic, or anything to make ornament loops
  - Make sure it will lace through the size of the punched hole.
- Red, green, white, or holiday-themed beads that will lace onto the chosen string size above

Necessary Equipment

- Scissors
- Hot glue gun
- Metal bottle cap hole punch
  - Try EuroTools or BCI Crafts brand—found on Amazon.com or in craft stores.

STEP-BY-STEP INSTRUCTIONS

Preparation

- Buy a variety of holiday/kawaii stickers that will fit within the 1-inch circle space.
  - **Reminder:** These must be thin and flat so that the epoxy dot will properly adhere to the image.
- Save a variety of copyright-free kawaii/holiday images to your computer.
- You can even make your own kawaii holiday images on Canva.com.
  - Make a free account with your e-mail address.
  - Click "Create a Design," then "Custom Dimensions."
  - Input 100 × 100 pixels, then click "Create new design."
  - Select "Elements" from the left side menu, and click on "Circle" under "Shapes."
  - Use your mouse on the corner of the inserted circle to drag the size to "w:96 h:96," which means 96 pixels and that it will print as a 1-inch circle.
  - You can then adjust the background color or transparency of the circle.
  - Search for "Christmas," "Holiday," or "Winter" in the left side search bar. Select "Graphics" to narrow down your search to transparent items that will fit in the circle.
    - » In my opinion, there is no need for the paid version of Canva if you don't already have access to it—a lot of the available free holiday images are pretty kawaii already!
  - When you've finished your 1-inch circle design, click the download button in the top right corner (the down arrow) and save the file as a .jpg. You can then insert the circle multiple times over into a Microsoft Word or Publisher document or continue to more circle designs. I recommend putting a lot of circles onto one Publisher page so you're not wasting paper.

- Or you can print off 1-inch bottle cap circle templates filled with copyright free kawaii holiday images.
  - Google "free 1-inch circle template" and save your chosen template image.
  - To create a fillable circle template, insert the saved image in Microsoft Publisher.
  - Click on Insert > Shapes and then click on the circle.
  - Draw circles on top of each templated circle shape, using the template as your size guide.
  - To fill each circle with a different picture, click on the circle > Format > Fill Effects > Picture > Select Picture, then browse through your folders to find your previously saved kawaii images for insertion.
- Print off blank versions of that same 1-inch bottle cap circle templates for decorating freehand with art supplies.

PROJECT INSTRUCTIONS

- Creators arrive and select their bottle caps.
- They can then decide if they want to create their own image in a blank circle template, or if they'd like to cut out a preprinted circle image, or if, perhaps, they'd like to use the given tiny stickers.
- Remind creators that they are decorating the underneath/inside of the bottle cap.
- Once creators have cut out their 1-inch circle designs (hand-drawn or computer printed), they will need to be hot glued to the bottle caps (have staff complete this portion for younger children).
  - If using stickers only, hot glue shouldn't be necessary.
  - Apply hot glue to the bottle cap itself in a quick, swirly motion, taking care not to create a large uneven lump, before carefully pressing the paper circle to it.
- Creators can now carefully place a glitter layer if they desire—larger flat glitter pieces work best and should ideally be glued down (a tiny dab of white glue can work for this instead of a hot glue bead) as well.
  - **Please note:** If glitter is left unglued, the epoxy dot from the next step won't stick to the circle image. It might be possible without gluing if the glitter use is very fine and sparing, but it's better to be safe and not waste the dot if it doesn't end up sticking.

- Carefully place the clear epoxy dot on top of bottle cap design.
  - No glue needed here—the dot is sticky enough. Glue will only create a foggy coating on top of the design, making it less visible.
  - Try not to touch the sticky bottom of the epoxy, as fingerprints can also be visible through the sticker.
- It's now time to punch the holes in the bottle cap with the tool. Take care to have it right in the top-middle of the wavy edge and to create two side-by-side hole punches in the top center to create a centered thread loop.
- Thread string, elastic, or cord through double holes.
- Adorn string with holiday-colored beads if desired.
- Tie a bow at the top of the string, and it's ready for the tree!

LEARNING OUTCOMES

Participants will . . .
- Learn how to use jewelry-making tools like the metal hole punch.
- Use their art skills by drawing unique kawaii designs.
- Learn a cheap and easy way to create homemade gifts.

RECOMMENDED NEXT PROJECTS

- If you have leftover supplies from your new bottle cap jewelry-making kit, chapter 31, Bottle Cap Jewelry, should be super simple!
- For more kawaii jewelry projects, check out chapter 33, 8bit Art, and chapter 36, Decoupage Tile Mini Masterpieces.

8bit Art

CHANTALE PARD

Youth Services Librarian, Keshen Goodman Public Library

8BIT ART HAS library patrons taking kawaii pixelated patterns and transferring them onto pegboards with plastic beads (often called "Perler" or "Hama"). Passing an iron over these beads fuses and melts them together so kids and teens can make adorable coasters, hair accessories, or magnets.

Age Range	Type of Library Best Suited For
Tweens (ages 8–12) Young adults (ages 13–18)	Public libraries

Cost Estimate

- $50
- **Cost note:** Although the initial cost of this program might seem high—these supplies should let the program run multiple times over, with little to no cost in the future—pegboards are reusable, as are large parchment paper rolls, and the bead quantities themselves go quite a long way. Kids and teens are often happy to make their melty creations just as is too, so if the key rings/barrettes/magnets run out, just go without.

Figure 33.1 | Sailor moon wand magnet, pink domo, and Kawaii heart keychain made out of Perler beads

OVERVIEW

This project should take a full hour, although it can depend on the size of the pattern. If creators finish their projects early, allow them to make more! Put on some fun background music while people work away at their melty artwork.

Creators will select their patterns, mine all their numbered bead colors from the buckets, and fill their pegboard according to paper patterned templates before having a staff member melt it together with parchment paper and an iron. Affix to a magnet/key ring/barrette, and they're ready to show off the newly created cuteness!

Materials List

- Perler or Hama beads
  - These can be purchased in giant mixed rainbow tubs, color-sorted kits, or individual packs of specific colors.
- Perler/Hama pegboards
  - These also come in 12-board packs of large assorted board shapes, which are great for group or class projects.
- Parchment paper
  - **Note:** Parchment paper is different than wax paper. Wax paper will melt to your beads and leave a torn paper film stuck to your project—not cute!
- Magnets

- Blank barrettes
- Key rings
- Embroidery thread

Necessary Equipment
- Iron
- Hot glue gun
- Small bowls or paint trays

Optional Equipment
- Tweezers
- Perler beads sweeper
  - This is for easy cleanup of dropped beads.

STEP-BY-STEP INSTRUCTIONS

Preparation

- Print off some kawaii Perler patterns from the Internet. Try looking for chibi anime or Sanrio characters, Pusheen, miniature fruits or sweets, or anything with that adorable sparkly eyed face.
  - **Pro kawaii tip:** you can anthropomorphize and kawaii-ize just about anything by adding your own sparkly anime eyes and smile to an item!
  - Pinterest and Kandipatterns.com have lots of options to search through. The latter even has a DIY pattern template.
  - Note that pegboards come in different shapes—the most common are the circle, square, or diamond. Be sure to only print patterns that are usable with the available board type.
  - If time allows, count how many beads of each color are necessary for each pattern and write it on your printout. Kandipatterns.com will normally already include this in their printout options, which is a helpful time-saver.
- Set up an iron on a table or counter that is less accessible to younger creators. Turn it on dry, at a medium setting, so it starts heating up during the peg-filling portion of the program. Remind all attendees not to touch the iron.

PROJECT INSTRUCTIONS

- Have program attendees choose their pattern.
- They can then select their beads for their project—it's best to make sure there are enough beads of the preferred colors before committing to a pattern. Hand out small paint trays or bowls for creators to keep their bead collections in while working on their projects.
- After mining all bead numbers and colors, creators can choose their corresponding pegboard.
  - **8bit tip:** I like to hand out pegboards only once someone has all their beads collected. Some patterns might be smaller than others, and you wouldn't someone with a giant pattern hogging the only circle pegboard for 15 minutes while mining for all their beads—it's likely that the smaller pattern selector could finish using the board while the other person is still mining. If you've got a smaller group with lots of boards, though, this may not be an issue for your program.
  - Keep in mind that mixed-colored-bead collections will draw out the time of this bead-mining portion of the program.
- It's now time to place all the beads on their pattern-corresponding pegs. Remind creators that counting the number of pegs over to their start spot will help steer them in the proper direction.
- Creators who are looking to turn their projects into key chains, necklaces, or anything requiring a hole should remember to leave one or two beads out of the pattern near the top-middle of the project.
- When the time comes to iron the beads together, have the creator *carefully* move the completed pegboard over to the staff ironing station.
  - **8bit tip:** stress the importance of slow, careful movements here because the slightest jostle can toss unironed pegs out of place. I recommend getting the creator to do the moving so there aren't any hard feelings if the staff member is the one who drops the project and wastes 30 minutes of peg placing time. (It happened to me once and ended with a 12-year-old in tears—I've still never forgiven myself!)
- Staff should then carefully place a piece of parchment paper on top of the beads before ironing them together with soft, slow circle motions. Again, take care not to jostle beads off their pegs.
- When beads look sufficiently fused together, gently peel the parchment paper and creation off the pegboard. Cover the back half of the project with parchment paper and make sure to fuse that side together with the iron too.

- Peel parchment papers off the project, and set aside to cool for a few minutes.
- Once the project is cool to touch, add the desired accessory: Hot glue a barrette or magnet to the back, or place a string through the top hole to create a necklace, ornament, or key ring.

Figure 33.2 | A Kawaii Luigi barrette

LEARNING OUTCOMES

Participants will . . .
- Learn how to follow a pixelated pattern.
- Use their fine-motor skills and hand-eye coordination.
- Practice their math skills.

RECOMMENDED NEXT PROJECTS

- Perler/Hama patterns are really just pixel art. Try having teens create their own Perler patterns by bringing out laptops and having them create their own digital pixel art, which can then be used as a template for their Perler project.
- Pixel art patterns also work in cross-stitch projects. Try expanding to this medium next!
- Increase the STEAM and coding learning by getting a Kano Pixel Kit—this $90 kit lets you build and code dazzling pixel pictures in more than 16 million colors.
- Why not create a day-long pixel camp where kids can try each of the above projects all in a row? Pump up the learning by providing a brief discussion about the history behind pixels (think retro video game art—maybe even have a few retro video games on hand to demonstrate!).

Bubble Pendants

MARY JARVIS ROBINSON
Adult Services Librarian, Novi Public Library

MAKING BUBBLE PENDANTS is a popular, fun, and attractive way to switch up your traditional arts and crafts programming and diversify your audience. The added bonus is that making fun and fashionable wearable art is an easy and fairly inexpensive project providing a lot of bang for the buck!

Age Range	Type of Library Best Suited For
Tweens (ages 8–12) Young adults (ages 13–18) Adults	Public libraries School libraries

Cost Estimate

Estimated to be about $2.50 per person. The cost will depend on whether supplies such as glue, alcohol inks, Mod Podge, and paper punches are already in the supply closet.

OVERVIEW

This craftastic kawaii program runs for an hour and a half. Attendees can socialize and try out several of the unique bubble pendant options that are

Figure 34.1 | Examples of completed bubble pendants; on the left, there are cut-out photos and images. On the top right, there are melted crayon pendants. On the bottom right, there are alcohol ink pendants.

provided. This program can be run with just one instructor; however, you will want to limit the size of the session to about 25 attendees. Step-by-step instructions with illustrations can be printed out ahead of time and left for participants on tables.

Materials List

Most materials can be purchased at the dollar store and Amazon.com.
- 1-inch pendant trays—round and square
- 1-inch glass cabochons—round and square
- Mod Podge
- E6000 glue
- Paintbrush, rolling pin, and tweezers
- 1-inch paper punches—circle and square
- Protective gloves
- Aluminum foil
- Alcohol inks
- Rubbing alcohol
- Crayons
- Hot plate
- An assortment of images, old books, magazines, old cards, postcards, and scrapbook paper

Optional Materials

- Small fume extracting fan. However, this is not necessary if the room has a usable window or is well ventilated.
- Hair dryer

Figure 34.2 | Supplies for bubble pendant program

STEP-BY-STEP INSTRUCTIONS

Preparation

- Use Google Images to find fun, whimsical images that appeal to a broad range of people as well as those customized to your region by having local sports team logos, maps of your city or state, or even your library's logo. Insert them into a document and scale them to 1 inch (1-inch diameter for round pendants and 1 square inch for square pendants). Card stock paper works best. Be sure to check the usage rights in Google Images so as to avoid copyright infringement. Also, attendees can be encouraged to bring copies (instead of originals) of personal photographs to be used. They must fit within the 1-inch parameter though.
- Create sample pieces in advance.

PROJECT INSTRUCTIONS

- After selecting a pendant tray, attendees can choose their desired image. If using a personal photo, the subject has to fit within the 1-inch parameter of the tray with a little room to spare around the edges.
- Once the image is cut to size with a punch, attendees will thinly coat both sides with Mod Podge. This step keeps the solvent-based E6000 craft glue from causing colors to bleed. If there is an overly zealous application of glue, a hair dryer can be used to dry out soggy pieces.
- After the dried image is adhered to the bottom of the tray with a dot of Mod Podge, a glass cabochon is glued on top with E6000. Use a small pea-size amount of glue, enough to spread to the edges. This step is tricky because too much glue can spill over and too little can cause visible air pockets. Also,

be careful because E6000 needs to be ventilated. This is resolved by using a small fume extractor or opening a door or window to ventilate the room.

- Alcohol ink on foil is another popular technique to make vibrant pendants. Alcohol inks are vivid, fast-drying pigments available in many hues. After smoothing flat a piece of crinkled foil, coat it with rubbing alcohol. Then the colorful alcohol ink is applied in random drops and gentle squirts from the bottle. As the inks blend together, luminous, jewel-like patterns emerge. After the foil dries, select a color pattern and cut it out with the hole punch. Follow the step above to finish the pendant.
- Another technique to try is using melted crayons. Crayon chips and shavings are arranged in the metal pendant tray and placed on a hot plate. The colors blend as they melt. Once liquid, swirling effects can be made by using a toothpick to "draw" through the colors. **Please note:** Participants need to work quickly before the wax bubbles up. The wax can be hardened quickly by placing it in the freezer for 20 minutes. Afterward, a glass cabochon is glued on top. The domed glass nicely magnifies and enhances the patterns.
- Colorful ribbons and cords are a cost-effective way for attendees to wear their artwork out the door.

LEARNING OUTCOMES

Participants will . . .

- Have an opportunity to socialize and share during this fun, interactive program (many enjoyed telling each other about the subjects of personalized photographs).
- Learn a few new techniques, such as using Mod Podge and alcohol inks on aluminum foil.
- Impress their family and friends with beautiful and fun wearable art they made themselves.

RECOMMENDED NEXT PROJECTS

Participants will find that this technique will apply to making key chains and bottle cap jewelry and refrigerator magnets, so be sure to check out chapter 31, Bottle Cap Jewelry.

35

Tiny Top Hats and Fascinators with Laser-Cut Felt Cameos

ANDREA HERMAN
Library Specialist, Saint Paul Public Library

TINY TOP HATS sit in the center of a Venn diagram that includes anime fans, Goths, and steampunks. They are common in Japanese Goth Lolita fashion, a style inspired by Europe in the eighteenth and nineteenth centuries, featuring frilly dresses and lots of accessories. This project combines tradition and technology—an old-fashioned cameo made with a laser engraver. Each attendee will leave with their own unique top hat or fascinator made by combining the cameos with feathers, ribbons, and appliqués.

Age Range	Type of Library Best Suited For	Cost Estimate
Young adults (ages 13–18) Adults	Public libraries	$130–$175

OVERVIEW

At the Saint Paul Public Library, we presented the tiny top hats and fascinators at our teen anime clubs and at a costume-making event at our Innovation Lab makerspace for the one hundredth anniversary of the George Latimer Center Library. This program would be good for a costume-making in the run-up to Halloween or to make cosplay for the local anime or comic convention because it creates a polished finished project without the need for sewing or jewelry-making expertise. The program typically lasts 90 minutes. Two staff members are ideal, but one is sufficient. It is recommended that you limit the group size to 12–15 participants so that you can show each individual attention. The cameos can be made ahead of time, or you can have them cut during the class and patrons can glue them together. Allow two hours if cutting time is included.

Figure 35.1 | Finished tiny top hat

Materials List

- White stiff felt
- Black stiff felt
- Card stock
- E6000 craft glue
- Tiny felt top hats (can be purchased from craft wholesalers such as Factory Direct Craft)

- Feathers
- Fabric or paper appliqués such as flowers or bows
- Ribbon
- Barrettes

Optional Materials

- Fabric covered headbands
- Black tulle circles

- Needle and black thread
- Hot glue guns

Necessary Equipment

- Laser engraver

- Scissors

STEP-BY-STEP INSTRUCTIONS

Preparation

- Cut the outline of the face and the frame of the cameo on the laser engraver using the black stiff felt. Cut circles from the white stiff felt to represent the inside of the cameo. The circles have to be big enough to glue the black frames on but not so big that the edges are visible.

- Feel free to use my patterns available here: www.dropbox.com/sh/ xey73d5sdk7yps1/AABMFByqwcFjbnoHZgIecRy9a?dl=0 or https://bit .ly/2RXrDZz.
- Cut circles in card stock the same size as the white felt circles to make the back of the cameo.
- Glue the white felt circle and the black felt frame to the card stock with a drop or two of E6000 craft glue.

PROJECT INSTRUCTIONS

- Decorate the hats as desired with cameos, ribbons, feathers, and appliqués. If you don't have enough E6000 glue for the decorations, hot glue should work. If you use the tulle circles for veils, sew them in with needle and thread.
- Glue two barrettes on each side of the bottom of the hat with E6000 glue. For extra staying power, barrettes can be snapped onto a stiff headband. A sturdy cloth ribbon can also be glued with E6000 on each side of the bottom of the hat and tied around the chin.
- To make fascinators, glue a rectangle of felt onto the barrettes with E6000 craft glue to use as a base. Decorate as desired.

Figure 35.2 | Felt cameos

LEARNING OUTCOMES

Participants will . . .
- Learn that the laser engraver is not just for wood and acrylic.
- Get their first taste of making their own costume pieces.
- Learn that they can create a design using public domain clip art and a laser engraver to make a charm from scratch.

RECOMMENDED NEXT PROJECTS

- Cameos can be used as pins, on bow ties, as pendants for chokers, and more. Combine the gears from steampunk gear earrings discussed in chapter 37, Laser-Cut Steampunk Gear Jewelry, for more Neo-Victorian fun!
- Patrons could bring in a picture and use a photo-editing program such as Photoshop or GIMP to make a silhouette for a personalized cameo.
- Use felt for larger costume pieces such as masks or eye patches.

36

Decoupage Tile Mini Masterpieces

ANDREA HERMAN

Library Specialist, Saint Paul Public Library

AS A CHILD of the '70s, I learned decoupage alongside string art and macramé, and it still has a special place in my heart. There is something special about combining bits of paper with some white glop that is both glue and varnish at the same time and transforming it into something completely new. Mod Podge is also water soluble for easy cleanup, lasts a long time, and can be used for many other projects. I have done this project three times with maximum attendance each time and my 32-ounce bottle is still half full.

Decoupaging tiles is an easy, cheap way to recycle magazines or withdrawn graphic novels. Patrons can see the library making good use of withdrawn materials instead of simply throwing them away. It is also a way to introduce older crafters who are familiar with decoupage to the joys of a laser engraver. As someone who cannot cut a straight line under any circumstances, making a lot of the same shapes quickly and evenly is an underheralded aspect of laser engraving.

Age Range	Type of Library Best Suited For	Cost Estimate
Young adults (ages 13–18) Adults	Public libraries School libraries	$65–$120

OVERVIEW

This program will run approximately 90 minutes. One staff member is sufficient for a group of 12–15 participants. Print card stock accent pieces ahead of time or during the program. Allow two hours if cutting and printing time is included.

For a teen anime or geek fandom club, have attendees find pictures of their favorite K-Pop stars or *Overwatch* characters to print out. Make sure you have a

Figure 36.1 | Completed tiles

4 × 4–inch template in an image editing program to ensure the picture is the right size. You could also print photos from a computer, but a laser printer is necessary, as ink-jet prints will bleed. When printing, use card stock to reduce tearing or wrinkling.

Materials List

- 4 × 4–inch tiles (tiles from the hardware or home improvement store are much cheaper than those from craft stores)
- Mod Podge
- Magazines/graphic novels or card stock
- Foam brushes
- Paper plates
- Paper cups
- Felt or cork (adhesive felt is more expensive, but it saves glue)
- E6000 craft glue

Optional Materials
- Laser engraver—preferred, but not essential
- Card stock for paper appliqués such as hearts, flowers, or frames
- Origami paper
- Mod Podge Clear Acrylic Sealer
- Command Strips
- Recycled paper or plastic bags

Necessary Equipment
- Scissors

STEP-BY-STEP INSTRUCTIONS

Preparation

- Cut the cork or felt on the laser engraver to the size of the tiles. Cut accent shapes such as hearts, flowers, or frames from card stock for decoration. If you don't have a laser engraver, you can cut the cork or felt with a hobby knife and the card stock with scissors or a vinyl cutter.
- The paper plates will be each attendee's workspace, which they can also use to carry their tiles home. Two or three patrons can share a cup of Mod Podge.
- Because the tiles are cheap, give each patron four tiles to make a set for coasters or hanging on the wall.

PROJECT INSTRUCTIONS

- Glue the cork or felt to the bottom of the tile.
- Brush Mod Podge on the top of the tile in a thin, even layer. A quarter-size drop of Mod Podge is enough for each layer. Brush once left to right and once up and down.

Figure 36.2 | Bottom of the tile with felt

- Gently place the pictures face up on the tile. If you have extra origami paper lying around, it makes a nice background. Gently press the pictures into the tile, starting from the center and working out.
- When collaging multiple elements, place them one at a time to keep them from drifting out of place. Apply the Mod Podge in a thin even layer on top of the pictures, wait a minute or two until it is tacky, and then apply another coat. Make sure each element has two coats.
- If the tiles are to be used as coasters, spray acrylic sealer after the tiles have dried for a few minutes. Using the sealer requires ventilation. Follow the instructions on the label carefully. Have the patrons stand back while spraying, then let the tiles dry for two to three minutes.
- If the tiles are to be hung as art, attach Command Strips to the back.
- The tiles should be mostly dry, but recycled paper or plastic bags can be used to protect them in transit. Wait 24 hours before hanging the tiles or using them as coasters.

LEARNING OUTCOMES

Participants will . . .
- Learn the principles of decoupage.
- Learn a creative use for their own recycled print media.
- Learn the convenience of laser engravers for cutting shapes quickly and evenly.

RECOMMENDED NEXT PROJECTS

- Decoupage containers such as boxes and tins for holiday presents.
- Decoupage an LED candle with handmade paper and appliqués for a one-of-a-kind minilamp.
- Patrons could bring their own photos and learn how to enhance them with photo-editing software, such as Photoshop or GIMP, and then print onto card stock and glue on tiles for display.

Laser-Cut Steampunk Gear Jewelry

ANDREA HERMAN
Library Specialist, Saint Paul Public Library

STEAMPUNK IS MORE than a genre combining Victorian style with futuristic technology, it is a lifestyle. Steampunks pride themselves in making their own unique costumes and props from scratch. When you see someone made their own animatronic parrot or light-up goggles, it can be intimidating, but this project is a way to try out steampunk style with an easy project that looks good and also teaches the very simplest way to make jewelry.

This project was inspired by seeing a wooden gear earring in a jewelry store and figuring out how to reverse engineer it, as my motto is "Never pay for something you can make yourself." I found the gear by searching "gear clip art" in Google's advanced image search and limiting it to public domain images, then adding a hole for the jump ring in CorelDraw.

At the Saint Paul Public Library, we presented the gear earrings at teen anime club and at "Tinker Tuesdays," a monthly hands-on maker program for adults. I wear them almost every day at work as a conversation piece to show patrons what can be done with the laser engraver in our Innovation Lab makerspace.

Age Range	Type of Library Best Suited For	Cost Estimate
Young adults (ages 13–18) Adults	Public libraries	$140–$200

OVERVIEW

This program will last approximately 90 minutes. Two staff members are ideal; however, one is sufficient for a group of 12–15 participants. Gears can be prepared ahead of time or be made during a class, as they cut fairly quickly. The sheets of wood could be painted ahead of time or left unpainted. Allow two hours if cutting time is included. If you paint ahead of time, it can be a good project for youth volunteers.

Materials List

- 3⅛-inch × 4-inch × 24-inch sheets of basswood
- Metallic acrylic paint in assorted colors (copper, gold, silver, brass, black, etc.)
- Brushes
- Mod Podge
- Cups for water and Mod Podge
- E6000 glue and applicator
- Flat metal gear charms in assorted colors to match paint
- Earring hooks
- 10- to 11-millimeter jump rings

Optional Materials
- Jewelry wire
- Round beads

Necessary Equipment
- Laser engraver
- Jewelry pliers

STEP-BY-STEP INSTRUCTIONS

Preparation

- Cut the gears out from the basswood using the laser engraver. Make sure to use the correct material setting.
- Feel free to use my patterns available here: www.dropbox.com/sh/xey73d5sdk7yps1/AABMFByqwcFjbnoHZgIecRy9a?dl=0 or https://bit.ly/2RXrDZz.

Figure 37.1 | Earring closeup

- Paint the gears on the top, bottom, sides, and inside the center hole. Leave to dry overnight.
- When they have dried, add a coat of Mod Podge and let dry overnight. This protects the paint and increases the shine of the surface.
- Make sure to identify the "front" side of the gear before using it. The "back" side of the gear will look flatter. The front side should always be facing out in any project.

PROJECT INSTRUCTIONS

- Glue one of the gear charms onto a small wooden gear with the E6000 glue. Glue the small gear onto a large one in a five o'clock position, making sure the spokes are pointing the same way for both gears. Contrasting colors for the large and small gear give a nice effect; each earring of a pair could also have opposite colors.
- Open the ring with jewelry pliers and insert it in the small hole of the larger gear.

- Insert the ring into the loop of the earring hook, making sure that the end of the hook is pointing in the opposite direction from the front of the gear. Close the ring.

Alternatively, you can connect the gear to the hook by wrapping jewelry wire around the hole in the gear, running the wire through a bead, and wrapping the wire around the earring hook.

LEARNING OUTCOMES

Participants will . . .
- Learn techniques they can use to make earrings from all sorts of beads and charms.
- Learn how a simple clip-art shape from the Internet can be imported into a design program to make a charm.
- Learn about steampunk culture and its DIY aesthetic.

RECOMMENDED NEXT PROJECTS

- Participants can create other jewelry with the gears, such as necklaces, bracelets, or pins. They can also adorn fascinators, hats, or ties. The possibilities are endless. At anime club, a teen once made a fidget spinner using nothing but gears and wire!
- Participants can use Google's advanced search to find their own public domain clip art to make into charms.
- Participants can create shapes in design software such as CorelDraw, Adobe Illustrator, or Inkscape and then cut the shapes to make charms.

PART VI

VINYL CUTTING AND STICKER PROJECTS

Vinyl Window Clings

LINDSEY TOMSU

Teen/YA Librarian, Algonquin Area Public Library District

WINDOW CLINGS CAN be a fun way to express individual creativity while showing off the things people enjoy the most! Participants of all ages can make window clings of their favorite things to hang in various places—windows, lockers, mirrors, and so on.

Age Range	Type of Library Best Suited For
Kids (ages 3–7) Tweens (ages 8–12) Young adults (ages 13–18) Adults	Public libraries

Cost Estimate

- Under $10 for a group of 50
- This cost is just for two rolls of vinyl cling. It does not include the cost of permanent markers, as many crafting supply closets may already have them on hand.

OVERVIEW

Who loves to decorate with vinyl or gel window clings? Lots of people of all ages! Who would like to decorate their windows, lockers, and mirrors with clings but is sad that most clings are mainly holiday-themed? Probably everyone who loves clings! Using simple static cling vinyl, participants can make window clings of whatever their hearts desire—animals, fandom characters, sayings, and so on. There is no limit to what can be made in cling form!

Most of my tween and teen programs run up to an hour and a half in length; however, this program could be done in as little time as 30 minutes. It also works great as a passive program where the supplies are just put out with a short instruction sheet! Some participants may feel apprehensive about their artistic abilities,

Figure 38.1 | Vinyl window cling made by the artist Sydney (on the left) for her friend Sarah's birthday (on the right)

but they don't need to fret—this program can be done with tracing! The program is very creativity-based, so one staff member on hand would be enough to monitor the program. Program budgets will dictate how many supplies can be purchased, which, in turn, dictates how many participants can attend. For $10 in supplies, this program can accommodate an average of 50 teens.

Materials List

- One or more rolls of Grafix Static Cling Sign Vinyl (available at Dick Blick Art Materials—www.dickblick.com)
- Permanent markers
    - If investing in new sets for this project, I recommend BIC Marking Color Collection 36-Count Assorted Sets of Fine and Ultrafine Tips (available at Dick Blick Art Materials—www.dickblick.com)
- Pencils
- Scratch paper

Optional Materials
- If a laptop can be in the room, include it! Participants who are not confident in their artistic ability can look up a design the library can print for them to trace.

Necessary Equipment
- Scissors

STEP-BY-STEP INSTRUCTIONS

Preparation

- The Grafix Static Cling Sign Vinyl comes in 27 × 36-inch rolls. Cut the rolls to size before the program. I recommend 5 × 5-inch squares. One roll of vinyl cut to this size will produce 35 squares along with 12 remnants (six smaller squares and six rectangular shapes that are still usable for small designs).
- The cling is attached to a paper backing that is just peeled off. Flip the roll over onto a long table and, using a yardstick, measure out the 5 × 5-inch grid and then cut. This size is large enough for participants to make one large-size cling or two or three smaller clings.
- At each individual seating space, place a pair of scissors, a pencil, and some scratch paper. At a common table, open the permanent marker sets and place those out for use. If using fine and ultrafine markers, try to keep the packs separate from each other and remind participants to return markers to their proper packs.

PROJECT INSTRUCTIONS

- As this program is creativity-based, show off any examples to participants before they begin. Encourage them to be creative and not feel like their final product must look exactly like the examples.
- Using the pencil and scratch paper, encourage participants to sketch out their design in a 5 × 5-inch square. There is no limit to what they can make into a window cling! If a laptop is in the room, allow participants to look up a design that can be saved to a Word document and printed. They can then just trace this design in the upcoming step. Simpler designs are better for beginners.

- When they have their design ready, show participants how to peel the cling from its backing (just like a sticker). Do not throw away the backing. It will be readhered to be transported home.
- Using an ultrafine-tip black permanent marker, trace the outlines of their design (from their sketch or a printed image) carefully holding the cling down to avoid smudges based on movement.
  - **Tip:** If participants are using a design with words on it, they need to be aware of how they are going to be adhering their cling to a surface. The back of the cling (the part that touches the paper) is the static part. If they plan to hang the cling so it is facing them (on a locker, a mirror, etc.), then they want to draw the wording on the front of the cling. If they plan to hang the cling so it is facing outward (a window looking outside, the inside of a car window, etc.), then they want to draw the wording on the back of the cling so the wording can be read from outside. If they have a hard time understanding this, use a window in the library to illustrate! Do they want to hang it on the window so *they* can read the message? Draw on the front. Do they want to hang it on the window so people *outside* can read the message? Draw on the back. Once they have their outline drawn, they can begin adding color. Use the fine-tip markers for large spots of color, while saving the ultrafine-tip markers for smaller areas of detail.
  - **Tip:** If participants are concerned about smudging their colors with the black outline, instruct them to flip the cling over to the side they did not draw the outline on and add color to that side instead.
- Once all the color is added to their cling, put it back on its paper backing, trying to line it up as perfectly as possible. If needed, use scissors to cut off any excess space or to separate multiple designs. The cling is now ready to be stuck in place!
- **Tip:** If, in the future, removal of the cling leaves behind markings on the surface, a little bit of rubbing alcohol will clean it right up.

LEARNING OUTCOMES

Participants will . . .
- Continue to develop creativity and imagination through hands-on crafting activities.
- Develop critical thinking skills by using disparate materials to construct a new item.

- Participate in hands-on crafting as creators, which enables them to participate in fun lifelong learning opportunities.

RECOMMENDED NEXT PROJECTS

- As mentioned, this program is a great passive program to be set out on a table during a holiday break or in a teen space. The library could even provide preprinted images of popular things for people to use as tracing designs.
- Vinyl clings are a creative way to teach participants about various types of art that go beyond just a paper and paint project. Participants can learn about stained glass windows and make a stained glass window cling, learn about pointillism and make a pointillism cling, or learn about graffiti as art and make a graffiti tag window cling.
- If the library has lots of windows that are often decorated during reading programs, consider buying a roll or two of cling and cutting out larger shapes. Invite members of the teen advisory board or other artistic volunteers to create large window clings for promotion of the programs.

Kawaii Planners

CHANTALE PARD
Youth Services Librarian, Keshen Goodman Public Library

KAWAII PLANNERS PUT an adorable twist on the recent "glam planning" fad. Make to-do lists, agendas, and homework notes all the more happy and exciting by spicing them up with a variety of stickers and washi tape. A student-driven task, this project should be easily suitable for all types of libraries.

Age Range	Type of Library Best Suited For	Cost Estimate
Tweens (ages 8–12) Young adults (ages 13–18) Adults	Public libraries Academic libraries School libraries	$20–$50

OVERVIEW

Program attendees should bring their own agendas/notebooks for decorating, but you can also print out a sample week's agenda spread for those who might wander in without their own supplies. Attendees can then get to work using your kawaii supplies to decorate a week or two of their agendas. You could keep the cost of this quite low if you stick to free printable stickers.

Materials List

- Kawaii stickers
  - These can be found at dollar stores, toy stores, craft stores, online, Asian markets, and so on.
- Washi tape
  - This can be found at Staples, craft stores, online, Asian markets, and so on.
- Printable sticker paper
  - Try 8.5 × 11-inch matte Staples Sticker Paper.
- Colorful gel pens
  - Gelly Rolls are gorgeous!
- Glam planning sample spread printouts
- Bullet journal sample spread printouts

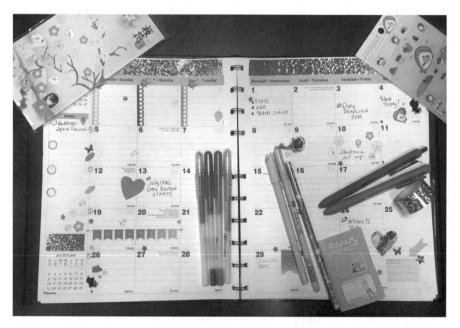

Figure 39.1 | This agenda has been Kawaii-fied by using some gelly roll pens, sparkly washi tape, and adorable stickers. Who wouldn't be inspired to be more productive in the face of all this cuteness?

Necessary Equipment

- Rulers
- Scissors (ideally enough for each attendee)
- Color printer

Optional Equipment

A Cricut or silhouette-cutting machine and associated printable sticker paper

STEP-BY-STEP INSTRUCTIONS

Preparation

- Buy a variety of kawaii sticker sheets—anthropomorphized fruit, kittens, unicorns, and so on.
- Buy a variety of washi tape.
    - **Note:** You can also find free printable washi tape for sticker paper online too.
- Print out a sample blank week's agenda spread.
- Print out sample bullet journal keys (legends).
- Download and print free printable kawaii sticker templates from your color printer onto your 8.5 × 11–inch sticker paper.
    - This can be done by searching "free printable planner stickers."
    - Planneraddiction.com has a lot of great variety.
- Have supplies out in the middle of the table, ready for everyone to share.

PROJECT INSTRUCTIONS

- Remind attendees to share all the stickers and leave some of each set for others.
- Have them look at the sample spreads and bullet journal keys, offering to help them create a version for their own to-do lists.
- Unless you're precutting stickers with a Cricut or silhouette machine, attendees will need to cut the preprinted template stickers on their own with scissors.
- Creators can then decorate their weekly spread however they would like
    - Gelly Rolls work well for bullet journal keys—I like to use a glitter pen for my bullet points.

- Washi tape often runs along the edges or separates sections as an adorable border.
- Encourage people to draw their own unique kawaii characters on their spread.
- Some printable planner stickers will be specifically shaped for a block-size according to name brand (see: expensive) planners. You can always take scissors to these stickers and cut them down to fit a specific area.
- Try printing out an entire 8.5 × 11–inch sheet of a pretty background pattern, so that creators can custom cut block sizes according to their needed fits. Use a ruler to measure the exact size.
- Decorate with prepackaged stickers throughout.

LEARNING OUTCOMES

Participants will . . .
- Learn the organizational technique of bullet journaling.
- Realize that organization can be exciting and fun.
- Learn how to make a simple, mundane task more aesthetically pleasing by expressing their creativity.
- Take home skills and ideas for how to continue the projects at home as a new hobby.

RECOMMENDED NEXT PROJECTS

- Incorporate kawaii journaling as an activity in your next self-care focused programming. Talk about the therapeutic benefits of writing down your goals and feelings, and have attendees try writing their own personal entries before decorating them.
- For more kawaii sticker projects, check out chapter 40, Create Die-Cut Chibi Stickers.

Create Die-Cut Chibi Stickers

SEE (PAIGE) VANG

Library Associate, Saint Paul Public Library

USING THEIR OWN art, participants will learn how to make die-cut vinyl stickers using the silhouette cameo machine.

Age Range	Type of Library Best Suited For	Cost Estimate
Young adults (ages 13–18) Adults	Public libraries Academic libraries School libraries	$5–$15

OVERVIEW

Patrons will learn how to set up files for use on the silhouette cameo machine as well as print super cute stickers and die-cut using the silhouette cameo machine.

Materials List

- Vinyl sticker sheets

Figure 40.1 | Vinyl-cut sticker on a travel mug

Necessary Equipment

- Silhouette cameo machine
- Computer with the silhouette cameo application, Silhouette Studio

STEP-BY-STEP INSTRUCTIONS

Preparation

- Help participants prepare their designs for use.
- Have sticker sheets ready to go.
- Have participants open the silhouette cameo application.
- Go to the "Page Setup" panel and turn on both the "Show Print Border" and the "Show Cut Border" options.

Project Instructions

- Have participants upload their images and also turn on their registration marks.
- Using the tool "Trace," trace the image area. This will outline and make cutting lines.
- If they want to design borders around the sticker, they should be using the offset setting.
- Cut away any trace inside the shape they want to cut out.
- To print the designs on the sticker sheets, do the following:
    - Set up cameo to white sticker paper.
    - Print and cut and send to silhouette.

LEARNING OUTCOMES

Participants will . . .
- Learn to use the silhouette cameo machine to make stickers at home.
- Learn to design their own sticker files along with border designs.

RECOMMENDED NEXT PROJECTS

- Participants may want to make stationery stickers or kiss cut stickers.
- Participants can create stickers for friends and family and for special occasions.

Kawaii Book Bag with Iron-On Vinyl

JAMIE BAIR

*Senior Public Services Librarian: Experiential Learning,
Fort Vancouver Regional Libraries*

PARTICIPANTS WILL USE Inkscape to create custom cute graphics ready for export to vinyl-cutting tools. They will watch their designs come to life as they are printed out and ironed on their own custom book bags.

Age Range	Type of Library Best Suited For
Tweens (ages 8–12) Young adults (ages 13–18) Adults	Public libraries Academic libraries School libraries

Cost Estimate

- $5–$50
- Inkscape is a free and open-source vector graphics editor.
- 10 feet of iron-on vinyl should cost $15–$25.
- Canvas bags should cost $1–$2 per bag (or participants can bring their own).

OVERVIEW

Participants will use Inkscape to design basic kawaii expressions. The resulting images are exported to vinyl-cutting software, such as Cricut Design Space or Silhouette Studio. This project can be completed by patrons with no prior graphic design experience. The graphics made in this project can be easily used for non-iron-on vinyl, paper crafts, and other activities.

Figure 41.1 | Super cute book bags

Materials List

Optional Materials

- Download the kawaii .svg files and detailed instructions from Dropbox: http://bit.ly/kawaiivinyl.

Necessary Equipment

- Inkscape software (download for free at https://inkscape.org/)
- Computer
- Iron-on vinyl (can be purchased at most craft stores or online)
- Vinyl cutter and software
- Iron
- Canvas bags, T-shirts, or other objects to kawaii-fy

STEP-BY-STEP INSTRUCTIONS

Preparation

- Project facilitators should check the vinyl-cutting software for acceptable file formats. Inkscape can save directly in many file formats as well as export to .png.
- Project facilitators should download and play with Inkscape before the workshop. The following tools are used in this project: creating circles, ellipses, and arcs; fill and stroke; align and distribute; transform; and group and ungroup.
- This project walks participants through the basic construction. Challenge participants to experiment with different shapes, designs, and elements to create unique designs.

PROJECT INSTRUCTIONS

This project follows basic kawaii design principles.
- Facial features are oversized.
- Facial features are aligned close to the center of the face.

Circle: The Base Shape

- Participants open a new project in Inkscape.
- Use the circle/ellipses/arc tool on the left-hand toolbar to click and drag to draw a basic circle.
- Switch back to the select tool (cursor arrow on the upper left) and click on circle.
  - Use arrow handles to resize object. Click on object again to activate rotating handles.
  - Open the Fill and Stroke window, Object → Fill and Stroke.
  - Set fill to black.

Eyes

- Draw a second smaller circle.
  - Set the size to 4 × 4 millimeters.

Figure 41.2 | Beginner Inkscape project

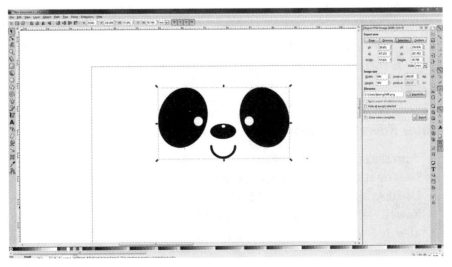

- Set custom sizes using the select tool, entering width and height measurements on the top toolbar.
- Using the select tool, click and drag a box around both circles.
  - Open the align and distribute window, Object ➔ Align and Distribute.
  - Align right sides and center on horizontal axis.
  - Change the smaller circle fill to white (pupil).
  - Use keyboard arrow keys to make fine adjustments to the pupil.
  - Select both objects and group, Object ➔ Group (Ctrl + G).
- Duplicate eye (Ctrl +D) and flip horizontal, Object ➔ Flip Horizontal.
  - Use the keyboard arrows to space the eyes evenly.
  - Align eyes on the vertical and horizontal axis.

Nose
- Duplicate the eye (Ctrl + D) and move to a blank space on the drawing.
  - Use the select tool and resize the eye to resemble a nose.
  - Delete the pupil or leave it for some shine!
  - Position the nose between the eyes.

Simple Smile
- Use the circle/ellipses/arc tool on the left-hand toolbar to click and drag to draw a basic circle.
  - Click on the circle still using the circle tool to select the circle's handle (right side of circle).
  - Click and hold the handle to change the circle into a half circle.
  - Open Fill and Stroke window, Object ➔ Fill and Stroke.
  - Set Fill to no paint.
  - Set Stroke paint to flat color.
  - Set Stroke style to width that produces a thick line.
  - Align smile on vertical axis with nose.

Other Kawaii Elements

- Turn the smile sideways to create eyelashes.
- Use the stars and polygon tool to add eye twinkles.
- Use the Clip tool, Object ➔ Clip ➔ Set, for an open mouth.
- Kawaii elements can be copy and pasted from the kawaii template available on Dropbox: http://bit.ly/kawaiivinyl.

Export File

- Check the vinyl-cutting software for acceptable file formats.
- Select all objects.
- Group, Ctrl + G.
    - File → Save As .SVG
    - File → Export .PNG
        » Export Selection
        » Pixels at ~300.00
        » Export
- The file is now ready to import into vinyl-cutting software.
- Tips on importing files to vinyl-cutting software are available on Dropbox: http://bit.ly/kawaiivinyl.

LEARNING OUTCOMES

Participants will . . .
- Practice using basic vector design software.
- Manipulate objects to create unique designs.
- Prepare vector image for vinyl cutting.

RECOMMENDED NEXT PROJECTS

- Chapter 39: Kawaii Planners
- Chapter 40: Create Die-Cut Chibi Stickers

Play in Darkness
Shadow Puppetry Meets Tech

AMELIA VANDER HEIDE
Supervising Librarian, Solano County Library

VINYL CUTTERS AREN'T just used to make clings and stickers. They can also help library users to create complex paper projects. In this program, teens will explore the history of shadow puppets and create one of their own using simple materials and one complex piece of technology. This project can be done on a simple level with each participant walking away with a cute shadow puppet of their own or can be rolled into a more complex project using film. In this project, teens will stop at their cool and, hopefully, cute shadow puppet.

Age Range	Type of Library Best Suited For	Cost Estimate
Young adults (ages 13–18)	Public libraries School libraries	$30–$50

OVERVIEW

This is a great program to do with teens who are interested in film (as it can be a preamble to stop motion), as part of a Lunar New Year celebration, or just because it's fun. I suggest building your program around a theme such as fairy tales, folklore, or even their favorite anime. Building your program around a specific theme helps to give your teens scope and ideas for their puppets. The idea is for teens to work in small groups of between two and four individuals to work through a story and create puppets that represent characters in that story.

Participating teens will learn about the history of shadow puppets and how to integrate a vinyl cutter into art projects. I suggest having three people help with this program. One person should serve as lead instructor, preferably a librarian or regular staff, and two volunteers or secondary staff members can help the teens. It is usually best to have one person per 10 participants. I have previously limited the size of this program to 20 participants. This is using two vinyl cutters and a computer for each group. It is recommended to host this program in a computer lab or on laptops. It should last approximately 45–60 minutes depending on participants.

Materials List

- Black cardstock
- Small-width wooden craft sticks (Popsicle size) or precut wooden dowels
- Glue sticks
- Wood glue
- Invisible tape
- Paper
- Pens
- Books or supplemental materials that are examples of your theme

Necessary Equipment

- Vinyl cutter (recommend at least one per 10 participants)
- Computer(s) with Internet access
- Scissors

Figure 42.1 | Finished unicorn puppet

STEP-BY-STEP INSTRUCTIONS

Preparation

Figure 42.2 | Vinyl-cut unicorn

- Set up your computer(s) and vinyl cutter(s). It is important to make sure they are working and you have Internet or Wi-Fi before starting.
- There are great videos available on YouTube to show teens examples of shadow puppets. Before starting the program, I suggest spending some time finding one you think your audience will enjoy. I recommend finding one representative of either China or Indonesia and one by Lotte Reiniger.

PROJECT INSTRUCTIONS

- Ask, "Does anyone know what a shadow puppet is?" "Why do you think people enjoy puppetry?" Listen to answers and encourage teens to participate.
- Read a brief history of puppetry.
  - Shadow play, or shadow puppetry, is an ancient art form with deep roots in Chinese and Indonesian cultures. In China, shadow plays are traditionally based on folktales and operas. In Indonesia, shadow plays are known as *wayang kulit*. These shows are deeply entrenched in Indonesian culture and are based on Hindu religious stories. The puppets used in these stories are traditionally made out of leather or wood. They are usually very intricate. In these plays, the puppeteer sits behind a white cloth with a backlight illuminating the puppets to create a shadow. A traditional *wayang* is very long and can last from 8 p.m. to 5 a.m.
  - The exact origins of shadow puppets in Europe are a little less clear. It is known that shadow puppetry was found throughout Asia and Asia Minor long before becoming popular in Europe. The art form began to

gain popularity in Europe in the eighteenth and nineteenth centuries. It became increasingly popular for children during the latter century. In the 1920s, silhouette artist Lotte Reiniger popularized the art form by using shadow animation to retell classic fairy tales, much like Walt Disney with hand-drawn animation would a decade later. Shadow puppetry is still enjoyed today, usually by children, throughout the Western world.

» Sources:
  o "Wayang." *World Book Student.* World Book, 2016. Web.
  o Scollon, John D. "Puppet." *World Book Student.* World Book, 2016. Web.

- Play videos for your teens. Ask them questions afterward, such as "What did you think?" "How do you think these are made?"
- Explain to teens that they will be making their own shadow puppets around a chosen theme.

Program

- Have students break up into groups of two to four participants.
- It is recommended to give each group a story or fairy tale to design their puppets around. Or if your teens have a favorite cartoon/anime, then have them use that as a jumping-off point for puppets.
- Have groups read through the story and choose three to four characters they believe are important in the telling of that story. They can use pen and paper to brainstorm.
- Once teens have chosen their characters, they will use their group's computer to either find images online or draw their own.
  – If drawing their own images, you can use the open-source software Inkscape to create solid-black images, or some vinyl-cutting software might offer their own design studio that will enable teens to draw within that space. I would only recommend doing this if you are willing to do a longer program or a multiday one. This is perfect in a classroom setting. However, for public libraries, I would recommend trying to find images.
- Teens can use Google to find images by searching the name of a character or object with the word "silhouette." For example, "unicorn silhouette" should give you solid black images of unicorns. You will need a solid black image in order for the vinyl cutter to cut around defined lines.

- Once teens have found or created the image they want to cut, have them upload the image to the vinyl cutter software. The type of machine varies from library to library. Make sure to show teens how to cut the image using your specific machine.
- Once teens have loaded and sized the image, cut the image onto black cardstock.
- When the image is done, use scissors to get any rid of any excess paper or bad cut-throughs. Attach the image to a wooden dowel or craft stick using one of the offered adhesives.
- Now each teen should have their own shadow puppet. Success!
  - If you wish, you can expand this into a longer program by having teens use their puppets to act out their story. You can also add complexity by trying to create moving puppets.

LEARNING OUTCOMES

Participants will . . .

- Learn about an ancient art form and its importance to cultures throughout the world.
- Expand how they can integrate technology into their craft and art projects.
- Want to, hopefully, use the vinyl cutter to create not just stickers but more amazing and complex paper art.

RECOMMENDED NEXT PROJECTS

- Chapter 38: Vinyl Window Clings
- Chapter 40: Create Die-Cut Chibi Stickers

PART VII

FOOD-THEMED PROJECTS

Deco Choco Pocky

CHANTALE PARD

Youth Services Librarian, Keshen Goodman Public Library

POCKY IS THE ultrapopular Japanese snack food that consists of a thin cookie stick dipped in a flavored chocolate. Chocolate, strawberry, and green tea flavors are widely available through the international food aisles in many North American grocery stores, whereas online retailers and Asian markets will also often have the more unique flavors like cookies and cream, chocolate banana, mango, and more.

Pocky can be seen in many an adorable anime scene, and some flavors even come in miniature heart-shaped sticks. It could be argued that plain Pocky already has a strong tie to kawaii culture. This project gets your creators pumping up the cuteness by decorating this yummy treat with candy melts and fun-shaped sprinkles.

Age Range	Type of Library Best Suited For	Cost Estimate
Tweens (ages 8–12) Young adults (ages 13–18)	Public libraries	$20–$60

OVERVIEW

This project works best as an activity to round out a larger program—it's unlikely your crowd of attendees will be able to occupy themselves with decorating

Pocky for an entire hour (and *if* they are able—they might go home with tummy aches). This is another project that I've often completed with my teen anime club—we'd decorate and eat some Pocky before watching an episode of our favorite show.

Deco choco Pocky can also be a great holiday activity—given that you can find so many holiday-themed sprinkles these days, it's quite simple to turn this into a quick festive treat or gift-making party.

Most Pocky boxes come with a couple to several individually sealed packages, each holding a few cookie sticks. If your budget allows, it's nice to give

Figure 43.1 | Kawaii Pocky decorated with candy melts and sprinkles

each attendee their own plastic package of Pocky, so they have a chance to try more than one design and even the possibility to make a matching set.

Materials List

- Pocky
- Candy melts
  - **Please note:** Candy melts are different than straight chocolate—they come in a wide range of colors and are much more easily melted. Try Wilton's or Mecken's brand.
- Variety of sprinkles (stars, hearts, sugar pearls, edible glitter, etc.)
- Ziploc bags
- Parchment paper

Optional Equipment
- Royal icing
  - The kind used for gingerbread houses can be a simpler substitute for candy melts.

Necessary Equipment
- Microwave

Optional Equipment
- Food-safe tweezers (for sprinkle placement)
- Wilton's Candy Melts Melting Pot

STEP-BY-STEP INSTRUCTIONS

Preparation

- Have each available seat prepped with a piece of parchment paper and a pack of Pocky on the table.
- Have plates of sprinkle options laid out on each table for sharing (include food-grade tweezers here if you have access to them).
- Prep candy melts: For each color, try 20 candy wafers in a sealed Ziploc bag in the microwave for 20 seconds. Carefully take the bag out and massage the melting candy before microwaving for another 10–15 seconds. Massage again, and repeat the 10-second process until the candy is completely melted.
  - If you're not comfortable microwaving plastic bags, you can place the 20-wafer color chocolate bags in a bowl of hot water before massaging them. Or if you've got a larger budget, try purchasing the $35 Wilton's Candy Melts Melting Pot.

PROJECT INSTRUCTIONS

- Have attendees choose their candy melt colors.
- Staff should snip the bottom corner of the plastic piping (Ziploc) bag—make sure it's extra small because you want it to fit on the thin Pocky stick.
- Make sure the bags are not too hot to handle—try wrapping them in paper towels if they are.
- Attendees can then use the piping bags to decorate their chocolate sticks:
  - A simple line of chocolate straight down the middle, with a few star sprinkles pressed on top
  - Drizzling several colors of chocolate on top
  - Coating the entire stick in a new candy melt color before rolling in finer sugar sprinkles

– Sticking several Pocky sticks together with the melted chocolate in order to create a larger chocolate backdrop area to decorate
- Set decorated Pocky aside on parchment paper to dry before taking a quick #kawaii Instagram photo shoot.
- Sit back and taste the yummy creations, or have attendees take some home in fresh Ziploc bags.

LEARNING OUTCOMES

Participants will . . .
- Learn how to use piping bags.
- Use their creative art skills for fine detail decoration.

RECOMMENDED NEXT PROJECTS

- In preparation for Valentine's Day, bring cute tissue paper and incorporate origami gift box folding in order to have attendees decorate Pocky projects as gifts to their loved ones.
- Try buying holiday-themed sprinkles and thematic colored candy melts for more festive Deco choco Pocky making.
- Use marshmallows on cake pop sticks for cheaper, yummy, kawaii choco fun.

Pocky Wars

MARISSA LIEBERMAN

Children's Librarian, East Orange Public Library

POCKY IS A delicious Japanese biscuit snack covered three-fourths of the way with chocolate and other flavors such as green tea, strawberry, milk, and cookies and cream. Pocky is a great snack to give out at anime clubs—my anime club tweens always ask for it! One of my favorite activities to do at my monthly anime club is Pocky decorating. While we watch anime, I encourage them to be creative, using frosting and colored sprinkles to decorate their snack. Pocky wars add a fun, competitive element to the more informal Pocky decorating program. Participants are split into small groups and have a set amount of time to create a cohesive kawaii or anime-themed entry.

Age Range	Type of Library Best Suited For
Tweens (ages 8–12) Young adults (ages 13–18)	Public libraries

Cost Estimate

- $25–$40
- Cost estimate can be scaled up or down depending on your sprinkle and frosting selections.

OVERVIEW

Pocky can be purchased at most Asian markets such as H Mart or through Amazon.com. You may also be able to find Pocky at Costco, Target, and chain grocery stores. For this program, it is recommended to purchase the packages of nine individually wrapped packs so patrons have their own set to decorate. Before Pocky wars begin, make sure to budget about 30 minutes for set up. This includes setting out Pocky and decorating materials, pouring sprinkles into bowls, and opening the tubes of gel frosting. Split your patrons into small groups of four or five, though the number of groups and people per group can be easily adjusted. This flexibility is especially important if you don't do sign up ahead of time. It's always great to have an extra staff member or volunteer on hand to assist, but it is not necessary for this program. Inviting staff in at the end as special guest judges is a fun way to introduce patrons to staff in other departments. This program is designed to last about 30 minutes plus 15 minutes of eating and cleanup. Pocky wars can take place within an anime club program or as a stand-alone event.

Materials List

- Pocky
- Variety of colored sprinkles
- Mini chocolate chips
- Mini gel frosting decorating tubes
- Plates
- Bowls
- Tablecloths
- Marshmallows or gummies for making creations stand up
- Small prizes for winning team (can be more Pocky!)

Optional Materials
- Microwave
- Chocolate melts
- Ziploc bag (for homemade frosting bag option)

STEP-BY-STEP INSTRUCTIONS

Preparation

- Cover tables with tablecloths.
- Set out plates, Pocky, and decorating materials.
- Create a sample.

PROJECT INSTRUCTIONS

- Split participants into small groups.
- Groups have 30 minutes to submit their entry.
- When time is up, invite guest judges to walk around to each group and score based on creativity, execution, and cohesiveness of entry. Invite participants to share what they created and how they came up with their designs.
- Make sure to get photos before the projects are eaten!

Figure 44.1 | Pocky wars at East Orange Public Library tween anime club

LEARNING OUTCOMES

Participants will . . .
- Be introduced to food from another country.
- Utilize teamwork and creativity.
- Utilize engineering components if they are building with the Pocky.

RECOMMENDED NEXT PROJECTS

- After Pocky wars, why not try making DIY Pocky to expand the program from decorating to baking? Search online for recipes.

Slow-Rise Squishies

ERIN DOUGLASS

Children's Librarian, Upper Saddle River Public Library

SQUISHIES ARE SOFT, tactile toys that originated in Japan and have exploded in popularity—such as adorable stress balls, typically food or animal themed. Think smiling milk cartons, colorful cupcakes, kitty hamburgers, anthropomorphized avocados, puppy-faced pieces of toast, and more. Their texture is immensely satisfying to manipulate, and some even smell good enough to eat. You may have seen them adorning the backpacks of students or lining the shelves of retail stores. This project will put a DIY spin on this kawaii craze by teaching tweens and young adults to create and decorate their own squishies.

Age Range	Type of Library Best Suited For
Tweens (ages 8–12) Young adults (ages 13–18)	Public libraries School libraries

Cost Estimate

- $100–$130 for approximately 25–30 participants
- $20 for a 20 × 20–inch sheet of high-density memory foam
- $80 for multiple sets of puffy fabric paints
- $10 for a bulk pack of disposable gloves

Figure 45.1 | Jumbo popsicle, mini popsicle, and a rogue doughnut

OVERVIEW

Participants will use fabric paints to transform a piece of memory foam into a super cute fidget toy that slowly reinflates after being squeezed to one's heart's content. No previous experience is necessary. Although gloves should be provided to save participants' hands from becoming as colorful as their creations, they should come prepared for messiness by wearing clothing they do not mind getting paint on!

This project works well as a one-hour session, though libraries wishing to provide a more individualized approach for participants can break the components into more than one session according to their needs.

One adult per 10 participants should be sufficient in most cases; teens will not need as much individualized instruction as younger tweens, so staffing should be considered based on the age group of participants. You may wish to either limit the size of the class or break a larger class into smaller groups with an adult staffing each table.

Materials List

- High-density memory foam—1–2 inches thick
- Dimensional puffy fabric paint—black, white, pink, and bright colors
- Jumbo craft sticks
- Craft sticks or makeup sponges for applying paint
- Paper plate—one for each participant to rest their work in progress on and use as a vehicle for taking their finished product home to dry
- Newspaper or plastic tablecloths for table covering

Optional Materials
- Hair dryer(s)

Necessary Equipment
- Scissors
- Thin-tipped paintbrushes for fine details
- X-Acto knife (if following the Popsicle template)
- Disposable gloves—one pair per participant

STEP-BY-STEP INSTRUCTIONS

Preparation

- With the exception of the memory foam and fabric paint, most of the materials and equipment can likely be found in your craft closet at no additional cost.
  - If you elect to use hair dryers to dry the thinner coats of paint faster, ask around—you may be able to borrow a hair dryer or two and/or bring your own. Just beware that it may end up with a paint smudge or two!
- Popsicle squishies are highly recommended for your first foray into this project as the shape is easy to replicate, and the Popsicle stick not only adds to the cuteness factor but acts as a handle for participants to grip while painting! The Popsicle shape can also be cut to include a bite mark on it, infusing additional outlets for creativity to be expressed through participants painting on the "filling" of their kawaii Popsicle. Find Popsicle templates and inspiration at https://tinyurl.com/kawaiisquishy.
- Decide on a set template. You may wish to draw the shape on the memory foam as a guide. Cut that shape out of the memory foam and trim its

edges for a smoother finish. Repeat until you have enough to provide one for each participant.

- Prime the base of the memory foam shape by dabbing white puffy fabric paint all over the surface with a makeup sponge or a craft stick. This will ensure that further painting is true to color and yield a final product that will rise slowly when squished. Leave plenty of drying time.
  - If you have the time, it would not hurt to apply multiple coats of white paint. The more layers, the squishier the end product will be!
- If you intend to create squishies other than a Popsicle, skip this step! Carefully use an X-Acto knife to cut a space in the bottom of the foam Popsicle shape to slide a Popsicle stick into. If the Popsicle stick looks too long for the foam shape, remove it and cut off the excess with scissors before pushing it back in. Use a hot glue gun to secure the Popsicle stick inside.
- Libraries wishing to accommodate more personalization by enabling participants to choose their own template can skip the advance preparation of cutting and priming the foam in favor of having participants tackle these steps as discussed above. This prep work should be covered in the first session, and the subsequent session should follow the directions outlined in the Project Instructions section below.
- Creating a prototype in advance is highly encouraged! It may be helpful to show this example to participants upon the start of the program. Besides being fun, the experience of making your own will help you to better see how the materials work together.
- On the day of the project, cover the workspace with newspaper or plastic tablecloths to prevent staining.

PROJECT INSTRUCTIONS

- Introduce the concept of the program, as well as how the fabric paint works in conjunction with the memory foam.
  - The thinner the layers of paint, the quicker it will dry.
  - The more layers of paint, the squishier the end product will be. Think of it as similar to painting your nails: It is better to apply multiple thin coats and dry them in between than to apply one gloppy layer.
  - Thin layers can be dried carefully with a hair dryer held at a distance from them.

- Thicker applications of paint will dry looking very puffy and three-dimensional so they look quite nice, *but* they take quite a long time (over the course of a day or so) to dry. This kind of application is best left for the finishing touches when the majority of the painting is done and cannot be dried with a hair dryer without causing the paint to run haphazardly.
- Show your example if you have decided to make one. Remind the tweens and/or teens that this is just a sample, not a rule book that they have to adhere to! Creativity is encouraged.
- Participants will first need to decide on a color scheme. Will it be primarily one color, aside from a kawaii face (should they choose to incorporate one)? Will it be multicolor in some way, such as icing or an ice cream filling?
- Show participants that they can mix paints with a craft stick on a paper plate to create lighter, pastel shades by adding white paint. For lighter colors like this, a little of the bolder, nonwhite color goes a long way. They can also mix other colors to produce their desired palette.
- After coming up with a rough color "map," instruct participants to use craft sticks and/or makeup sponges to dab on fabric paint of the predominant color(s) of their choosing.
- Their squishy-in-progress should ideally be kept on a paper plate while they are working on it.
  - If they want to paint the back of their squishy, they should do that side first in a sparing, thin layer of only one color before flipping it over to work on the front.
- Once participants have based out their foam shape in paint, they can choose areas that they want to be more puffy and three-dimensional.
  - For example, a squishy dessert's icing and sprinkles can be applied with generous applications of paint straight from the fine-tipped paint bottle at the very end of the project when it need not be touched anymore.
  - Sparkly kawaii eyes, blushing cheeks, and a mouth can also be added this way. For eyes, apply a circle of black paint from the bottle, and then apply a smaller circle of white paint using a thin-tipped paintbrush. For blushing cheeks, use a thin-tipped paintbrush to paint on round pink circles. A smile can be painted on carefully, directly from one of the bottles of black paint.

- At the conclusion of the program, be sure to remind everyone that their squishy creations need ample time to dry when they take them home. The final products will be super satisfying to squish but only after they sit on the paper plate for *at least* a day, ideally somewhere in the sun, such as by a window. You could also choose to set them aside in your crafting area, makerspace, or other appropriate room and allow participants to pick them up in a couple of days.

LEARNING OUTCOMES

Participants will . . .
- Learn that, given some guidance, inspiration, and supplies, they can replicate and reimagine things that they may wish to buy from a store.
- Gain experience with do-it-yourself projects and feel empowered to experiment further.
- Learn that there are a myriad of ways to use different materials.
- Think more deeply about the construction of objects.

RECOMMENDED NEXT PROJECTS

- Challenge yourself to make a variety of squishies in other shapes. If you have created Popsicle squishies, try doughnuts, cute kitty faces, or something totally out of the box!
- You may wish to try your hand at making a Kawaii Paper Squishy (chapter 18)!

PART VIII

CRAFT PROJECTS

Kawaii-Faced Polymer Clay Charms

SARAH SIMPSON
Youth Services Librarian, Westerville Public Library

CREATING THAT ADORABLE kawaii face in any medium can be a challenge for middle grade kids who are still honing their fine motor skills. In this clay project, map pins, a sip straw, and a little practice help create the perfect kawaii face on little critter charms. The end result is a kawaii charm that can become part of a keychain, necklace, or bracelet.

Using the outline of this sculpting process, you can create dozens of different kawaii critters and foodstuffs with minimal artistic talent or skill. Just a few simple tools (map pins and a sip straw) and some polymer clay can create the most adorable clay charms to adorn jewelry, phone cases, or backpacks.

Age Range	Type of Library Best Suited For
Tweens (ages 8–12) Young adults (ages 13–18)	Public libraries School libraries

Cost Estimate

- $2.50 per participant
- This is the cost of supplies that are most likely not readily available in your library's supply cabinet, such as the polymer clay, sip straws, jewelry eye pins, and map pins.

OVERVIEW

Because of the relatively minimal artistic skill required to create the clay charms, this could easily be a middle grade program, but teens will love it as well. You can increase the level of difficulty for teens by adding painted details after the clay is baked, but the program detailed here will be suited to ages eight and older.

Limiting attendance will ensure that everyone has enough supplies to create at least one charm. One adult to every eight kids is a good ratio so kids can ask questions and get guidance in the sculpting process.

Materials List

- Sculpey III Oven-Baked Clay Sampler, 1-ounce, 30 packages
  - This can be the polymer clay multipack of your choice, but I prefer working with Sculpey and find it to yield consistent results. I would suggest getting a multipack of many different colors so that participants can make a wide variety of types of charms.
- Small sip straws—these are the straws that are usually found in cocktails, any color
- Map pins (in black or the color of your choice)
- 1–2 centimeter jewelry eye multipack (gold or silver)
- 1-ounce bottle of Superglue
- 6-ounce bottle of acetone nail polish remover
- Small craft-only bowls

Figure 46.1 | Kawaii-faced polymer clay charms

- One small, synthetic paintbrush for each participant
- Toaster oven with tray (two if your program size is larger than 10 participants)

Optional Materials
- Small brush for detail painting
- Jump ring/key chain
- Acrylic paint
- Polyform Sculpey Gloss Glaze—this would be applied after baking and would air dry to form a glossy coat

Some of these supplies will likely be on hand in your library or at home (acetone-based nail polish remover, map pins, sip straws, and toaster oven), whereas others require special purchase. Each charm requires about a half ounce of clay, and in the recommended multipack, each color could produce two charms. The most challenging part of the project is creating the kawaii face. Once participants create one successfully, they will easily be able to create a second (or third). I would recommend baking all the charms together, but baking time is relatively short, so staggering the bakes could be done in a one-hour program.

STEP-BY-STEP INSTRUCTIONS

Preparation

There is little to do beforehand to prepare for this project. Each participant should work at a table and have a workstation set up for him or her. The workstation should include access to a small amount of acetone (poured in small disposable cups or craft-only sharing bowls), a paintbrush, a selection of map pins, and a precut sip straw. The sip straws will need to be cut in half on one end to form a semicircle end (see figure 46.2). This semicircle will create the kawaii mouth on the charm.

PROJECT INSTRUCTIONS

- The shape and the face are the same regardless of whether your participants decide to create a kawaii orange, cat, bear, bunny, guinea pig, dumpling, egg, or meatball. The sky is the limit with round items.

- Encourage participants to think of this charm as a series of easy shapes stuck together. Start by creating a round ball of clay measuring approximately 1 inch in diameter.
- Add details to your charm by using a separate piece of clay to sculpt small ears (pointed for a cat, pointed and long for a rabbit, rounded balls for a bear) and feet. The feet consist of four very small pieces of clay rolled into balls and then squished flat to form discs.
- To create the kawaii face, insert two map pins for the eyes. The best placement for the eyes is about ¾ inch apart on the equator of the charm body.

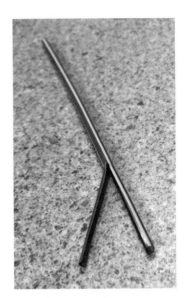

Figure 46.2 | Cut sip straw

- Affix the details (ears, tail, feet—all optional) to the large ball by brushing a small amount of acetone nail polish on the two areas that you would like to adhere. Press the details on firmly.
- Insert the precut sip straw twice to create the rounded "w" shape. The mouth should be positioned either in between the two map pin eyes on the equator or slightly below the equator and centered in between the eyes (see figure 46.1).
- Insert the jewelry eye pin at the top of the charm, opposite the feet.
- Bake the completed kawaii charm on a tray in the center of the toaster oven for 12 minutes at 275 degrees. I have found that this will create a firm, durable cure on the charm without warping the plastic on the map pins. If you are worried about warping, you can remove the plastic map pins with tweezers prior to baking and reinsert them once the charm is cooled.
- Once the charm is cooled to the touch, remove the jewelry eye pin.
- Apply superglue to the eye pin and reinsert it into the charm. This will ensure that the eye pin does not fall out of the clay charm. A small amount of superglue is required for this so participants can share a bottle.

LEARNING OUTCOMES

Participants will . . .
- Use basic rolling and imprinting techniques to create a truly adorable work of art.
- Gain experience using polymer clay (this material doesn't require special equipment to cure, comes in a rainbow of colors, and can be used to create a wide range of art projects).

RECOMMENDED NEXT PROJECTS

- Kawaii polymer beads: Create large polymer beads with kawaii faces for an eye-catching statement necklace or bangle.
- Create kawaii doodle transfers on polymer clay. Draw a doodle with colored pencil and paper. Lay the doodle face down on an unbaked polymer clay sheet and transfer by applying light pressure with the backside of a spoon. Bake the transferred doodle. Add color with permanent markers.

Poké Ball Terrariums

ERIN DOUGLASS
Children's Librarian, Upper Saddle River Public Library

SINCE THEIR CREATION more than two decades ago, Pokémon are still everywhere. Their popularity continues to grow, running the gamut from children to tweens, teens, and even adults. The adorable pocket monsters occupy a trading card game, video games, manga, and cartoons. With more than 800 "species" and 18 "types" (such as fire, ice, water, grass, psychic, and ghost), Pokémon are as diverse as their fan base. The augmented reality app *Pokémon Go* took the world by storm, transposing pocket monsters onto the real world for players to "catch" in a Poké ball. What if we could turn the concept that has captured the imagination of many into a tangible object? In this project, participants will create a scenic home for a Pokémon within a transparent Poké ball.

Age Range	Type of Library Best Suited For
Tweens (ages 8–12) Young adults (ages 13–18)	Public libraries School libraries

Cost Estimate

- $150–$330 for approximately 12 participants
- $15 for plastic fillable ornaments
- $10 for white acrylic paint

- $10 for scenic spray glue
- $12 for mason jar lid rings
- $15 for peel-and-stick moss
- $20 for miniature trees
- $5 for terrarium rocks
- $5 for landscape snow
- $5–$10 for each Pokémon mini figure
- $5–$10 for each battery-operated wire light string (optional)

OVERVIEW

In this project, tweens and teens will compose a circular, 3-D scenic landscape that will be housed in the clear top half of a fillable ornament. The scenery will be tailored to the Pokémon and its characteristics, forming an adorable Poké ball habitat that its owner can see into. Although the beginning steps of the project will be uniform for all, participants will have a chance to express their creativity by selecting a Pokémon and composing the makeup of their landscape base. Lights can be incorporated to add a glow to the Poké ball's atmosphere.

Figure 47.1 | Alolan Vulpix, an ice-type Pokémon, in its snowy Poké ball habitat

This project will take up to an hour and a half, depending on how immersed participants become in the landscaping process. For a group of 12 participants, two staff members would be ideal. It is best for a smaller group so that everyone participating can receive personal attention and direction if they need guidance, but increasing the number of adults staffing the project would allow libraries to accommodate a larger number of tweens and teens.

Materials List

- Clear plastic fillable ornament, 100 to 140 millimeters—one for each participant
- White acrylic paint
- Cardboard
- Peel-and-stick moss sheets
- Scenic spray glue
- Landscape snow
- Miniature plastic Pokémon figure—one for each participant
- Miniature trees, shrubs, foliage, rocks, and so on
- Mason jar lid ring—one for each participant
- Newspaper or plastic tablecloths for table covering

Optional Materials
- Loose packs of moss in a variety of colors and textures
- Acrylic paints and paintbrushes to alter the color of rocks or other additions—this will add more time to the project, partly due to drying time
- Battery-operated wire light string with batteries included—one per participant
- Any other miniature decorations you wish to add—the terrarium/fairy garden/diorama section of craft stores such as Michaels offer many accessories, such as benches, mushrooms, campfires, and so on

Necessary Equipment
- Hot glue guns and hot glue sticks—low-temperature hot glue guns are ideal
- Paintbrushes
- Nail clippers
- Nail files
- Scissors

STEP-BY-STEP INSTRUCTIONS

Preparation

- Because there are so many Pokémon, enthusiasts often feel very passionate about their favorites and not-so-favorites. As such, advance registration is recommended; take this opportunity to include a section that asks registrants to choose between the Pokémon figures that will be available. This will be a huge help in deciding what mini figures you need to buy. Just make sure that you only offer Pokémon choices that you will be able to obtain the mini figure of. Some are much easier to find and more affordable than others.
- The Poké ball will be made of two halves that snap together. Because the bottom half needs to be white, you may carve extra time out of your program by painting the bottom halves with white acrylic paint in advance.
- Cover the workspace with plastic tablecloths or newspaper to ensure that no paint or glue stains the tables. This will also make cleanup a breeze!

PROJECT INSTRUCTIONS

- The clear, fillable plastic ornaments that will become a Poké ball have two parts: a top half and a bottom half that interlock but can be separated. You will want to have the ornaments already interlocked to form a full dome when you hand them out so that everyone has a top and bottom that fit together. Instruct participants to open up their clear plastic ornament by gently pulling them apart.
- These domes are meant to be ornaments that can be hung by threading a piece of string through the nubs. However, you do not need these pieces of plastic that extend outward. There will be a "nub" on each half of the clear plastic dome. Participants will use nail clippers to carefully trim off this excess plastic on both halves of the ornament.
  - Although these nubs can be trimmed off cleanly, you may want to have your tweens and teens use a nail file to carefully file down any bump that has been left behind. Remind them to be gentle because the clear plastic the ornament is made of can scratch or break if they are rough with it.
- You want the Poké ball to have a clear top half and a white bottom half. Have participants use paintbrushes to paint one half of their clear dome

with white acrylic paint. They can apply multiple coats until it looks mostly opaque. Once they are satisfied, participants should set aside this half of the dome to dry.

- Have tweens and teens place the other half of the dome on the cardboard with the hollow part face-down and trace it with a pencil. Then they will need to use scissors to cut out the circular shape they have traced. Because the cardboard circle they will end up with will be slightly larger than the circumference of the ornament, they should trim it slightly to ensure that it will rest comfortably inside the hollow of the ornament. They can trim, place it in the open space of the clear ornament half, and repeat until it is a good fit.
  - Think of it like a sandwich: The two ornament halves will be the slices of bread, and the cardboard circle will be the filling.
- Participants can set aside their clear ornament half because they will need to focus on the fun part: creating the scenery of their Poké ball habitat. They can take a piece of the peel-and-stick moss sheet, trace their cardboard circle onto the nonmossy back side, and cut it out with scissors. Have them peel off the backing of the moss sheet and carefully adhere it to the cardboard circle so that they match.
  - It will be helpful to show them that they can line up the edges first and smooth it down that way.
- Once they have their terrarium moss base, participants will take a more individualized approach with their layout. They can add loose moss, miniature trees, shrubs, rocks, and so on with a hot glue gun. Instruct them to try laying out their chosen additions first without glue to ensure that everything will fit comfortably. Also remind them to leave a space for the centerpiece of their Poké ball—the Pokémon!
  - If you are doing this project with tweens, you might decide to have staff members be in control of the hot glue guns.
  - If you decide to let the tweens use the hot glue guns firsthand, demonstrate how to apply hot glue carefully and never near their fingers so that they do not burn themselves. Remind them that it takes a little time for it to dry: Until it cools into a solid glob of glue, it will be hot!
- Though miniature trees *are* miniature, some might be too tall and will need some trimming to the bottom to fit; show them how to judge the size against the height of the clear ornament half by holding them up against one another.

- For participants who want to make a Poké ball for an ice-type Pokémon, show them how to spray adhesive glue onto the areas of their terrarium base where they want to include snow, sprinkle landscape snow on it, and then add another mist of the spray glue. Be sure to tell them that it will take a few minutes for this to dry.
- Participants will decide on a spot for their Pokémon plastic mini figure and set it down in that location to double-check that it is to their liking and then add hot glue to the bottom of the figure and press it firmly into place. Instruct them to hold it down for about 10 seconds or so to make sure that it takes hold securely.
- Instruct participants to check that the white, bottom half of the dome has dried, and then rest it inside a face-up mason jar lid ring. The hollow of the lid will keep the white half-dome from rolling away. Though not necessary, hot glue can be used to permanently attach them by lining the rim with glue.
- Participants will gently seat the finished terrarium base inside the hollow of the white half-dome. It should be comfortably snug, staying in place so long as it is handled with care.
- If you do not intend to include LED lights, skip this step. Show tweens and teens how to carefully coil the mini light strand around itself to fit inside the circular shape of the terrarium base. As long as you use a small wire light strand, it should be easy to form and bend so that it stays in place. It will be easiest to coil it so that it wraps around the very outer rim of the terrarium base. Participants will most likely need to coil the strand around several times to ensure that there is no "spillover."
  - Instruct them to leave enough of the battery pack end of the wire out of their loop of lights. The wire of the light strand will be flexible and thin enough to protrude out, allowing room for the battery pack to sit outside of the Poké ball, so that it can be turned on and off.
- With the bottom half complete, participants will need to attach the top. Show them how to line up the top and bottom halves, holding the bottom with one hand and carefully pressing the top half down with their other hand to snap them together. Their Poké balls are now complete!
  - If participants added LED lights, switch them on to see the dazzling light-up Poké balls. You might now want to shut off the lights and admire how they look in the dark!

LEARNING OUTCOMES

Participants will . . .

- Practice spatial thinking skills by arranging small objects to fit proportionately and compositionally.
- Create a scenic diorama-style terrarium with a landscape that suits the characteristics of their pocket monster.
- Learn how to make a craft that is endlessly modifiable and perfect for a personalized homemade gift.

RECOMMENDED NEXT PROJECTS

Next, try creating diorama terrariums in larger glass containers. You could tie a real-world habitat to the animal and plant life that coexist there and incorporate a discussion of ecosystems, sustainability, climatology, and so forth. For instance, you may want to make a desert scene in a mason jar with sand and other geographic features typical of that biome, as well as mini figures (store bought or created with polymer clay) such as cacti, snakes, tortoises, and so on. Participants could break into groups, each tackling a different biome or ecosystem.

Neko Atsume Fluffies

CHANTALE PARD
Youth Services Librarian, Keshen Goodman Public Library

NEKO ATSUME (OR "cat collector" in Japanese) is the free, addictive cat collecting app that has players placing food or toys in their virtual backyard spaces in an attempt to attract more adorable chubby kittens to their feline family. With a total of 64 collectible cats in a game (22 of which are considered rare), the app requires players to learn what cats like what treats enough to come join your group.

This viral app spawned a ton of kawaii fan art online, including the popular "Easy Fluffy Neko Atsume Pom Pom Tutorial" video, posted by YouTube Creator BudgetHobby in 2016. The Neko Atsume fluffy program below makes use of BudgetHobby's free template and tutorial to have your youth-filled room making their favorite Neko Atsume kawaii kitties.

Age Range	Type of Library Best Suited For	Cost Estimate
Tweens (ages 8–12) Young adults (ages 13–18)	Public libraries	$10–$20

OVERVIEW

Depending on how many pom-pom kitties each person wants to make, this activity could take up an entire 60-minute program time. Alternatively, staff could also round out the event with other kawaii kitty games.

Put out a couple of library iPads (if available) so that attendees can start playing the Neko Atsume app—perhaps the first cat they collect in a game should be a good recommendation for which fluffy pom-pom to make first.

Try creating a kawaii kitty trivia game with questions or pictures of well-known adorable cats: Pusheen, MitchiriNeko Marchers, Nyan Cat, Grumpy Cat, Chi's Sweet Home, Doraemon, Bee, and Puppycat, and other cats from anime or Western cartoons.

Materials List

- Yarn in a variety of colors (white, orange, yellow, black, brown, grey)
- Felt in a variety of colors (white, orange, yellow, black, blue, brown)
- Recycled cardboard

Necessary Equipment
- Scissors (enough for each attendee or a few pairs to share)
- Binder/bulldog clips (four per attendee or a few sets to share)
- Hot glue gun

Figure 48.1 | A finished Neko Atsume fluffy amid our Kawaii cat trivia prizes

STEP-BY-STEP INSTRUCTIONS

Preparation

- Print out color sheets of the full roster of Neko Atsume cats.
- If time allows, precut as many of the cardboard horseshoe shapes as possible.
- Print out several copies of BudgetHobby's free template, found in the description box of their YouTube video.
- Study the tutorial video and test out your own pom-pom or two to get the hang of how to clip the cardboard horseshoes and where to tie the two half poms together.
- If younger children are the intended audience for this program, think about decorating the room with different stations for portions of the craft process—like a "salon" table where wrapped pom-poms go to have their hair cut or the "eye/ear doctor" where they then go to have their felt pieces hot glued on by staff.

PROJECT INSTRUCTIONS

Creators should select what kitty they would like to make and select their appropriate horseshoe pattern and colored yarn.

- Staff should choose these as well and walk creators through the process with a demonstration.
- Example patterns include the following:
  - **Snowball/Socks/Smokey/Shadow:** Full-color cats use the plain horseshoe pattern.
  - **Ginger:** Cats with a small circle of a different color in the middle front face use the 40/20/40 on one side and the plain pattern on the other.
  - **Lexy/Sunny/Peaches:** Cats with a different top side corner (including ear) color can use the 30/70 pattern on one side and the plain pattern on the other side. The plain pattern should be the same color yarn as the 70 portion here.
  - **Pumpkin/Callie/Pickles:** Cats with a different colored top half of the face can also use the 30/70 pattern on one side and the plain pattern on the other side, but the plain pattern should be the same color yarn as the 30 portion here.

– **Spud/Bandit/Spooky:** Cats with multiple spots can use the 30/70 pattern on one side and the 85/15 pattern on the other side. The 70/85 portions should be one color, and the 15/30 portions should be the second color.

- **Please note:** Although not all cats are listed above, by looking at the visual list of cats, many should be easily modified by the switching of yarn or felt colors. For example, Smoky can easily change to Pepper with the simple replacing of one yellow eye for a blue.
- Creators can try recreating their own pet kittens by experimenting to see if they can figure out the division of color percentages for new cat patterns.
- Some of the 64 cats are unique in that they wear little accessories. Xerxes IX, for example, wears a yellow crown, a grumpy eyebrow, and a colored afghan. See if creators can make accessories out of the variety of provided felt.

LEARNING OUTCOMES

Participants will . . .
- Learn how to make quick and easy pom-poms for future crafts.
- Use their fine motor skills.
- Use their math skills in creating new kitten color patterns.

RECOMMENDED NEXT PROJECTS

- Try creating pom-pom bunting—prep all your pieces for several pom-poms, and instead of tying each together with a smaller separate piece of yarn, tie the whole group together on one large piece of string—perfect for kawaii bedroom or party decorations!
- For more kawaii kitty crafts, try chapter 49, MitchiriNeko March Hats.

MitchiriNeko March Hats

CHANTALE PARD
Youth Services Librarian, Keshen Goodman Public Library

THE MITCHIRINEKO MARCH is a viral Japanese YouTube video that has seen more than 11 million views. The video shows chubby, feather-hat-wearing, animated kittens conducting a marching band parade to a kawaii, addictive, ear-worm of a song. YouTube fan account Kipper even created a 10-hour loop of the adorable marching kitten video, which has seen an additional 2.1 million views itself.

The MitchiriNeko March program has children enjoying and studying this viral video and making their own marching hats before performing their own adorable version of a MitchiriNeko March around the library.

Age Range	Type of Library Best Suited For	Cost Estimate
Kids (ages 3–7) Tweens (ages 8–12)	Public libraries	$20

OVERVIEW

Because the program includes both practice and performance sections in addition to the crafting activity, it should fill a regular 45- to 60-minute time slot, depending on how large the group is.

Children arrive to the program and enjoy the MitchiriNeko March video as a group before making their own marching band hats with the help of staff, examples, and instructions. Hats should be wide enough that they can simply sit on a child's head, as opposed to needing any sort of tie-on string (avoiding a possible choking hazard).

Once hats are complete, staff can pass around percussion instruments—egg shakers, tambourines, triangles, and so on so that children can practice making music along with the song. After a short, casual practice on marching, the group will perform a MitchiriNeko March parade around the library, led by a staff member or teen volunteer.

Materials List

- Red cardstock (8.5 × 11–inch sheets)
- Plain white paper
- Jewels or light-green cardstock
- White glue
- Yellow feathers
    - Children can also create their own feathers with scissors and yellow paper or, if they aren't sticklers for details, could choose any other color feather.

Figure 49.1 | A finished MitchiriNeko March hat: shiny glitter style

Figure 49.2 | MitchiriNeko March video on YouTube

Necessary Equipment
- Scissors
- Stapler
- Paintbrush
- Class set of instruments (triangles, tambourines, egg shakers)
- Laptop/projector/screen
- Sound system

STEP-BY-STEP INSTRUCTIONS

Preparation

- Set up projector screen in program room, with MitchiriNeko March video ready to play.
- Set up sound system on library floor, with MitchiriNeko March ready to play during performance.
- Prepare a couple of premade sample hats to help inspire construction.
- Precut red cardstock into sheets that are 6 × 11 inches in size.
- Precut strips of white paper into strips that are 1 × 11 inches in size.
- Create a red-tassel baton and an adult-size version of the marching hat for the staff or teen volunteer who leads the final march performance.

PROJECT INSTRUCTIONS

Introduction

- Watch MitchiriNeko March video.
  - Ask children to keep an eye out for silly differences. One cat carries a duck on his head instead of a hat, one eats spaghetti, and another talks on a cell phone instead of playing instruments.

Hat Making

- Start by making a cylinder out of two sheets of the precut red cardstock, aiming for something that is 6 inches tall and 22 inches around. Staple together at the edges.
- Glue a band around the bottom of the cylinder using two strips of the precut white paper.

- Turn the cylinder facing frontward (with stapled seams on the sides) and glue a yellow feather near the top center.
- Glue a green gem (or a precut green cardstock circle) over the top of the bottom tip of the feather.

Parade Prep and Performance

- Pass out percussion instruments and have children practice shaking to the beat of the MitchiriNeko March.
- Demonstrate marching on spot, and have children practice marching and shaking to the beat of the music.
  - Depending on the age of the crowd, expectations should be kept low here for keeping things in sync. It's meant to be a fun activity, so staff shouldn't expect perfection.
- When the group is comfortable, children can put on their hats before staff start up the sound system music and lead them through a library marching parade to the MitchiriNeko music.
  - Desk staff might want to make a loudspeaker announcement when given a signal to warn other library customers of the temporary increase in noise (and to watch out for the adorable marching children).
  - If the group is collectively too shy to march around the library floor, try inviting the parents inside the room to perform it there as a continuous circle (although, lack of change in location may be less exciting).

LEARNING OUTCOMES

Participants will . . .
- Learn how to make quick and easy hat crafts at home.
- Experiment with musical instruments.
- Practice marching on beat.

RECOMMENDED NEXT PROJECTS

- Children could also make their own mini instruments after creating their hats—small conductor batons out of Popsicle sticks, tambourines with bells and paper plates, or shakers made out of rice, wax paper, and toilet paper rolls.

- Try scaling down the hat size in order to make miniature march hats for willing pets or stuffed toy cats. Creators can then take them home and put on the MitchririNeko March music in the background before taking a quick video clip of the kitty. They can even try marching around them in their own hats.
- For more kawaii kitty crafts, try chapter 48, Neko Atsume Fluffies.

50

Screen Printing

CHANTALE PARD

Youth Services Librarian, Keshen Goodman Public Library

SCREEN-PRINTING WORKSHOPS ARE engaging interactive art projects that can encourage library users to express their creativity, show off their fandom loyalty, dress in kawaii style, and even provide free promo for the library itself. Participants bring their own T-shirts for screen printing images that are preselected and prepared by library staff.

Age Range	Type of Library Best Suited For
Kids (ages 3–7) Tweens (ages 8–12) Young adults (ages 13–18) Adults	Public libraries

Cost Estimate

- $150
- **Cost note:** Although the upfront cost for this project might seem high, the Diazo Screen-Printing Kits will set you up for multiple screen-printing programs. When you run out of consumables like photo emulsion and ink, they are easily replaceable for $15–$30, and the lights/screens/squeegees should last for years.

OVERVIEW

It's unlikely that this project will occupy program attendees for a full hour—but it might take staff the entire 60 minutes to oversee the screen printing for each individual T-shirt. Have other related crafts and activities out in the room so people can keep themselves occupied while waiting for their turn to print their T-shirts.

When the time comes, creators approach the screen-printing table with a prelined piece of fabric. Library staff will place the screen on the desired area of the T-shirt and direct creators on how to pull the squeegee back and forth to press the ink through the screen.

Figure 50.1 | A young patron gets a glow-in-the-dark star printed onto their decorative pillow.

Materials List

- Apron
- Rubber gloves
- Heavy string to construct a clothesline
- Recycled newspaper
- Large piece of scrap fabric

Necessary Equipment

- Speedball Diazo Ultimate Screen-Printing Kit
- Speedball Advanced All-In-One Screen-Printing Kit (alternatively)
  - These kits cost around $150 and include everything you need to get started on screen printing: frames, squeegees, inks, emulsion fluids, transparency sheets, and even the lights and instructions for use. They can be purchased on Amazon or most art supply stores, such as Hobby Lobby and Michaels.
- Iron

STEP-BY-STEP INSTRUCTIONS

Preparation

- Be sure to remind attendees to bring their own light-colored fabric to the program in all relevant promotional materials.
  - Using white or a lighter-colored ink? Have them bring dark fabric instead.
  - T-shirts are ideal, but pillowcases or canvas bags will work too. If printing a pillow, remind creators that although the ink is nontoxic, the packaging does not say if it is tested for prolonged, direct skin contact. It's best to use pillowcases as a decorative option, as opposed to sleeping with their faces directly pressed against the ink.
- Be sure to select a copyright-free image for burning. Remember that the image print needs to be done in black—either a silhouette of an image or a thickly lined drawing. Consider the following options:
  - Have a staff or volunteer hand draw the image.
  - Text is always an easy choice—that is, "#KAWAII."
  - Search the Internet for "copyright-free silhouette" images.

- Try searching for "kawaii" or "cute" in Cricut Access if you have a Cricut machine and subscription to this service.
- You could alternatively print your own kawaii silhouette images on Canva. com.
  - Make a free account with your e-mail address.
  - Click "Create a Design," then "Custom Dimensions."
  - Input 8.5 × 11 inches (this should be suitable for the screen size that comes with the screen-printing kits noted above), then click "Create new design."
  - Search for "kawaii," "cute," "kittens," "unicorns," "fruit," and so on in the left-side search bar. Select "Graphics" to narrow down your search to items that you will more likely be able to change to solid black in color (some graphics allow you to change the color palette, but beware that some won't).
  - When you've finished selecting and editing your silhouette design, click the download button in the top right corner (the down arrow), save the file as a .jpg, and then print it. This will be the template to use when photocopying this image to the transparency paper (detailed instructions are in the screen-printing kit).
    » We like to print two copies of the transparencies to double up on the thickness of the ink when burning the image onto the screen—two transparencies stacked on top of each other makes for a heavier blackout to block light from poking through and creating holes in your image.
  - Alternatively, if you purchase or obtain the free trial of "Canva for Work" (which gives you free access to all the crown images), you will have a wider access to kawaii pictures, in addition to the kawaii faces, which you can insert over any inanimate object to make look adorable.
  - If you go the free trial route, make sure to download as many kawaii images as you can while you have access—this way you'll have a back stock for the next time you run the program instead of having to pay for access.
- Read screen-printing kit instructions thoroughly, and start the screen burning process at least a week before the program proper. The process should only take a few hours, but it can also take a few tries to get the hang of, so you won't want to leave it until the last minute.
- Tack paper print outs of all available images to a visible wall in the program room.

- Staff should wear protective gear—aprons and rubber gloves—or, if not, at least items they might not mind ruining with new ink smudges.

PROJECT INSTRUCTIONS

- Creators arrive and decide what image they'd like to print onto their fabric (if there is more than one option—our branch has a good hang of the screen-burning process, so we like to offer two or three image options when doing a screen-printing program).
- Have people line the inside of their T-shirts or pillowcases with one or two recycled newspaper sheets so the ink doesn't transfer through to the other side of the fabric.
- Explain to attendees that staff will be printing one image at a time with a specific color of ink.
  - Preselect appropriate ink color per image. Or, if there is a small variety, have the crowd choose what color is best for each design.
  - It's best to print one image at a time because once ink is pressed through the screen, it will start to dry. If staff were to press one image and then set that screen aside for 20 minutes, the ink can start to dry and create patchy spots in the burned image on the screen. Washing ink off the screen prematurely can also increase the chance of removing emulsion and likewise ruining the image.
- Creators can then approach the staff printing table and help select where on their fabric they would like to print the image.
- Under staff instruction (usually one person needs to hold the frame down tight, whereas the other is the squeegee runner), creators will press the ink through the screen in order to create the kawaii image on their fabric. Two squeegee passes will usually do, if pressing firmly: once toward yourself, once away from yourself, and perhaps a third time in the opposite direction by the staff member to ensure the proper pressing pressure.
- Carefully remove screen from fabric—creators should hold fabric down flat while the staff person carefully lifts up the screen and places it to the side on some recycled paper.
- It's best to then have a second staff member or volunteer on hand to iron the image. Carefully cover the fresh ink with a piece of dry scrap fabric and iron over top. This heat will help set the ink more quickly, as will tossing the fabric in the dryer when they get home.

- Further, recycled newspaper will be useful for creators who leave directly after printing their T-shirts. They can use a piece as a barrier over the fresh inked image to roll up the T-shirt for easy transport home.
- For creators who are sticking around to do more prints, crafts, or even just hang out at the library, it's best to have a space ready for placing drying T-shirts. Think about creating a clothesline in the program room, or carefully lay T-shirts over the backs of chairs (ink image facing up).

LEARNING OUTCOMES

Participants will . . .
- Learn how to recreate the screen-printing process at home.
- Try their hand at using the squeegee.
- Express their kawaii style by adding a new, unique piece of clothing to their wardrobe.

RECOMMENDED NEXT PROJECTS

- Try purchasing acrylic screen print ink (for use on paper, as opposed to fabric) and use it for art projects where creators screen print a basic kawaii outline onto cardstock before decorating around it with additional art supplies.
- Hold a community art contest where artists submit their line drawings in advance. Select finalists, and have branch regulars vote on their favorite image. Burn the winning design onto the screen to use during the next screen-printing program.

51

Carving Cute Critters

SARAH HUBER

*Assistant Professor of Library Science and Engineering Technology
Information Specialist,
Purdue University Library of Engineering and Science*

ALYSSA EDMONDSON

*Libraries Instructional Developer,
Purdue University Library of Engineering and Science*

ROBIN MEHER

Library Assistant, Purdue University Library of Engineering and Science

AT THE PURDUE Library of Engineering and Science, we use our maker events as a way to let students know what we have available to them. The carving cute critters project demonstrates subtractive CNC technology and gives students an opportunity to paint and talk to their library faculty and staff in an informal, fun way.

With carving cute critters, students are given precarved blocks of wood to decorate with painter markers. We use the Inventables Carvey machine and their free software, Easel, but any CNC carving machine with compatible software works for this project. This is a layered activity. Participants can either decorate woodblocks and see how a tabletop CNC carving machine works or take it a step further and create their own cute critter to be carved. We have found this to be one of our most successful events. Students are focused on painting the blocks and ask questions about the machine. We are thanked for offering the event and asked when we will hold it again.

Age Range	Type of Library Best Suited For
Tweens (ages 8–12)	Public libraries
Young adults (ages 13–18)	Academic libraries
Adults	School libraries

Cost Estimate

- Approximately $80–$100
- This does not include initial cost of a CNC machine.

OVERVIEW

This project is best to host over a few hours, allowing people to come and go. Some students go through the project quickly, but we have found the majority spend time adding details. This program can be run by anywhere from one to three staff members. Librarians can introduce themselves, let participants know about the library resources and then take a step back and let them draw, only giving directions if they want to design a cute critter that will be carved. Although you may not have to limit the number of students painting on the blocks, you may want to limit those designing their own cute critter to two at a time if you have only one carving machine.

Materials List

- (3) ¾-inch × 6-inch × 6-foot pine boards that are cut into 5½ inch × 6 inch at the hardware store at the time of purchasing the boards
- Paint markers (you can use paint, but the paint markers don't leave a mess to clean up)
- Paper for students to draw
- Black felt tip markers, a range in thickness

Optional Materials

- We always have out washi tape because students seem to love it and apply it to just about any project we offer.

Necessary Equipment

- Tabletop CNC carving machine—we use the Inventables Carvey
- Two computers—either laptops or tablets, whatever you have available that has an Internet connection and that allows you to download the CNC software

Figure 51.1 | Painted carved cute critters

- CNC Software that connects to your CNC carving machine if you are letting students design a drawing to be carved (We use the Inventables free, web-based software and free software download.)
- Wet/dry vac with HEPA filter to clear shavings from CNC carving machine
- Access to a printer/scanner

We chose the Carvey because the company ensures that fumes stay within the hood. That is what makes it portable. If you are working with a different CNC machine, where exhaust is a concern, or if you do not have a tabletop machine, you may have to think about just doing the woodblocks. You could also host two sessions: one where you have students do the drawings, then you have them carved, and a second session for drawing their blocks that have been carved.

STEP-BY-STEP INSTRUCTIONS

Preparation

- Set up two long tables with chairs and place precarved cute critter blocks, painting markers, and paper with felt-tipped markers for drawing.
- Set up one small table with computers to use CNC software.
- Set up one small table with tabletop CNC carving machine.
- Place the vacuum next to the table with the CNC machine on it.
- Set up event close to a printer/scanner to scan the images students draw.
- Set up a flat screen next to the event with a slide show showing your mobile making logo and then examples of painted woodblocks (optional).

PROJECT INSTRUCTIONS

Figure 51.2 | Hand drawings and carved cute critters

- As students walk by to their classes, ask if any would like to paint woodblocks.
- When students come over to the tables, show the woodblocks they can paint. Because we are limited with how many students can design their own cute critter, we wait to see if students show a deeper interest. If they do, then we show them the steps to design their own cute critter.
- If a student chooses to draw their own cute critter, show them predrawn examples to demonstrate the importance of keeping the drawing simple and the lines legible and well defined. If there is a lot of detail, shading, and/or thin lines, there is a good chance the carving will not turn out. Keep it simple.
- After students have made their drawings, scan them, and e-mail them to their e-mail address.
- Once they receive it, they can download it to the desktop or another storage of their choice and save it as .jpg, .png, or .gif. The image resolution as the scan works fine.
- Students then need to register for a free account with Easel, which is web-based and anyone can sign up for it, not just someone who has purchased a Carvey. There is other free CNC carving software available. It is best to see what your machine's company recommends.
- For Easel, go to the Inventables site and select "Explore Easel," where you will be prompted to start a new account or sign in.
- Once in the software, select your machine at the top of the screen. Carvey and X-Carve machine have different dimensions.
- Select "New Project."
- Select the "Import" tab on the menu bar at the top of the grid screen.
- Select "Image Trace" and upload your scanned drawing.
- Manipulate the image as needed using the "Threshold" and "Smoothing" sliders, and then click the green "Import" button.
- The drawing will show up on the gridded design plane.

- If using Carvey, adjust your image to be clear of the red corner, which shows where the wood goes into the clamp.
- Choose your desired cut depth, drill bit size, and material. For our projects, we always work with pine, choose "Soft Maple" from Easels material choices, and work with either 1/32 or 90-degree V-bit.
- Download the Easel plug-in, or choice of software, to your computer. For Easel, the download is available at easel.inventables.com/downloads.
- Connect USB from Carvey to computer or tablet.
- Once your CNC carving machine is connected, prompts will appear in the software to make sure all the entered settings are correct—for example, the type of material, material placement, and that the clamps are holding the material in place.
- Start carving.
- Simple carves are typically between 5 and 20 minutes.
- If students cannot wait for their carved cute critter, they can come back to the event later and paint them, or they can pick up their piece at a designated library service desk at a better time for them.

LEARNING OUTCOMES

Participants will . . .
- Produce a cute critter woodblock through their painting.
- Design a cute critter hand drawing to be turned into a carved cute critter woodblock.
- Observe how subtractive technologies and manufacturing can begin with a simple hand drawing.

RECOMMENDED NEXT PROJECTS

- A group can coordinate a number of colored blocks to create a hanging collage that represents where science, art, and technology meet.
- Blocks can be cut, colored, or stained to create a structure, or individual structures, through gluing or attaching with fasteners of choice.

Polymer Clay Charms

Youth Services Coordinator, Caledon Public Library

POLYMER CLAY IS a simple and fun way to create your own kawaii charms! This versatile medium is easier to use and manipulate and less messy than other clays! With an abundance of straightforward step-by-step tutorials available on YouTube and other websites, participants can find inspiration online or come up with their own unique creations.

Age Range	Type of Library Best Suited For
Tweens (ages 8–12) Young adults (ages 13–18)	Public libraries

Cost Estimate

- $40+
- Costs are dependent on the number of participants and amount of clay that you need to purchase.

OVERVIEW

Polymer clay charms are a great program to let participants be creative and express themselves! This program works well as either a registered event or a drop-in activity. For registered events, we typically limit participants to 20 tweens or teens and buy enough clay for each participant to make three to four charms each during the course of an hour. For drop-ins, we specify that the program will only last until materials run out and limit the creation of

Figure 52.1 | Kawaii polymer clay charms

charms based on the size of the crowd that shows up. Only one staff member is required in both situations in order to demonstrate the various tools that the participants can use and help them with any minor creation complications.

Materials List

- Polymer clay (the softer the clay the easier it is to work with)
- Liquid polymer clay
- X-Acto/craft knives
- Acrylic roller

- Detailing tools (come in packages at craft stores)
- Eye pins
- Baking sheet

Optional Materials
- Tiles
- Acrylic paint
- Paintbrushes

- Chalk pastels
- Polymer clay glaze

Necessary Equipment
- Oven

STEP-BY-STEP INSTRUCTIONS

Preparation

- Print out images of polymer clay charms to help inspire participants.
- Have various YouTube video tutorials set up on tablets or laptops for participants to view for inspiration.
- Practice making some charms of your own, and display your finished products for participants to view. These can also be used to create a display advertising your program in-house!

PROJECT INSTRUCTIONS

- Once participants have an idea of the kind of charm that they would like to make, they should start by cutting off an appropriate amount of clay in the color that they require. Make sure to instruct attendees to start off with small amounts, as only a little bit of clay is necessary to make charms, and they can easily add more clay as needed.
- Participants will need to condition the clay by rolling it in their hands to warm it up and make it easier to work with.
- Once the clay feels easy to mold, they can begin shaping it into their preferred design.
- Tiles can be used if desired for cutting, rolling, and shaping the clay, as it does not easily stick to the surface.
- When adding smaller details that stick out from the charm (ears, tails, wings, etc.), use the liquid polymer clay to stick the pieces together like glue.
- Detailing tools can be used to add texture to the charms and makes the placement of smaller objects, such as eyes and mouths, easier to manage.
- An optional method of adding more color to charms is to brush on a dusting from chalk pastels.
- Once participants are happy with the shape and detailing of their charms, add the eye pins before placing them in the oven on a baking sheet while following the clay's baking instructions. Most charms only take between 12 and 15 minutes to bake.
- After the charms have cooled, participants can glaze them to add a nice sheen or add some acrylic paint details if desired.

LEARNING OUTCOMES

Participants will . . .
- Develop their skills at shaping and manipulating an art medium that may or may not be familiar to them.
- Foster and cultivate their creativity.

RECOMMENDED NEXT PROJECTS

- Chapter 53: Polymer Clay Magnets
- Polymer Clay Photo Holders
- Polymer Clay Tic-Tac-Toe Board

Polymer Clay Magnets

NATALIE SPAAN
Youth Services Coordinator, Caledon Public Library

POLYMER CLAY IS a medium known for its ease of use and ability to appeal to both children and teens alike. These kawaii magnets are one such example where designs can be as simple or complicated as the creator desires! Younger kids can use cookie cutters to make their shapes, whereas older tweens and teens may wish to freehand their own creations.

Age Range	Type of Library Best Suited For
Kids (ages 3-7) Tweens (ages 8-12) Young adults (ages 13-18)	Public libraries

Cost Estimate

- $40+
- Costs are dependent on the number of participants and amount of clay that you need to purchase.

OVERVIEW

As in the case of the polymer clay charms, these magnets work well as either a registered or drop-in activity, with minor staff assistance required. The

Figure 53.1 | Kawaii polymer clay magnets

only limiter on the size of your program is the amount of clay that you can afford to purchase for participants to use. Due to the ease of this activity, it does well as an hour-long program itself, or as a smaller part of a larger program like anime clubs, comic con events, or themed storytimes. When run as a registered program focused only on the creation of the magnets, I try to purchase enough clay for each participant to make three to four magnets over the course of an hour.

Materials List

- Polymer clay (the softer the clay the easier it is to work with)
- Liquid polymer clay
- X-Acto/craft knives
- Acrylic roller
- Detailing tools (come in packages at craft stores)
- Magnets
- Adhesive (i.e., E6000)
- Baking sheet

Optional Materials

- Tiles
- Acrylic paint
- Paintbrushes
- Chalk pastels
- Polymer clay glaze

Necessary Equipment

- Oven

STEP-BY-STEP INSTRUCTIONS

Preparation

- Print out kawaii images to help inspire participants.
- Practice making magnets of your own, and display your finished products for participants to view. These can also be used to create a display advertising your program in-house!

PROJECT INSTRUCTIONS

- Once participants have an idea of the kind of magnet that they would like to make, they should start by cutting off an appropriate amount of clay in the color that they require.
- Participants will need to condition the clay by rolling it in their hands to warm it up and make it easier to work with.
- Once the clay feels easy to mold, roll using an acrylic roller as if it is cookie dough until it is evenly spread and at least 1-inch thick. The clay can be rolled on top of tiles if desired, as it does not easily stick to the surface.
- Participants can then use cookie cutters to create a cute shape for their magnet or use a craft knife or detailing tool to freehand their own shape.
- Once the general shape of the magnet is complete, participants can get creative and decorate their designs using more clay or the detailing tools.
- When adding smaller details that stick out from the magnet (such as ears, tails, wings, etc.), use the liquid polymer clay to stick the pieces together like glue.
- Detailing tools can be used to add texture to the magnet and make the placement of smaller objects, such as eyes and mouths, easier to manage.

- An optional method of adding more color to the magnets is to brush on a dusting from chalk pastels.
- Once participants are happy with the shape and detailing of their magnets, place them in the oven on a baking sheet and follow the clay's baking instructions. Most charms only take between 12 and 15 minutes to bake.
- After the magnets have cooled, participants can glaze them to add a nice sheen or add some acrylic paint details if desired.
- To complete the project, don't forget to add a magnet on the back using a strong adhesive such as E6000.

LEARNING OUTCOMES

Participants will . . .
- Develop their skills at shaping and manipulating an art medium that may or may not be familiar to them.
- Foster and cultivate their creativity.

RECOMMENDED NEXT PROJECTS

- Chapter 52: Polymer Clay Charms
- Polymer Clay Photo Holders
- Polymer Clay Tic-Tac-Toe Board

RESOURCES AND SUPPLIES

Here are some places to acquire supplies, find patterns, take tutorials, and gain inspiration for all sorts of crafting projects.

PATTERNS

Etsy

This immense website dedicated to offering handmade items from crafters around the world is a fantastic resource for craft supplies. You'll find everything from polymer clay and resin molds to patterns for felties and crochet to vinyl cutter files for download. Here are just some of the markets dedicated to craft patterns:

- www.etsy.com/c/craft-supplies-and-tools
- www.etsy.com/market/craft_patterns
- www.etsy.com/market/feltie_pattern
- www.etsy.com/market/vinyl_cutter
- www.etsy.com/market/crochet_patterns
- www.etsy.com/market/quilling_patterns
- www.etsy.com/market/jewelry_patterns
- www.etsy.com/market/beading_patterns
- www.etsy.com/market/polymer_clay_pattern
- www.etsy.com/market/polymer_clay_mold

Thingiverse

The Thingiverse website has more than 1.3 million 3-D models that are shared within the community. They are available for free download.

- www.thingiverse.com

Tutorials and Inspiration

Amino

Amino is a mobile social network for handmade crafters; the app can be downloaded for free from the app store on mobile devices. This is a place to connect with the crafting community and gain inspiration.

- https://aminoapps.com/c/crafty

YouTube

There are hundreds of thousands of crafting tutorials on YouTube. Conducting a search for "kawaii" plus the medium you're interested in working with, such as "polymer clay," along with "tutorial" will provide you with plenty of resulting instructional videos.

- www.youtube.com

Instructables

This website is run by Autodesk whose catchphrase is "make anything," and there are plenty of tutorials to be found therein to back up that claim. A search for the term "kawaii" returns page after page of step-by-step tutorials for craft projects, all available for free.

- www.instructables.com

Pinterest

More than 175 billion ideas are shared on Pinterest, many of them craft ideas. A search for "kawaii craft ideas" will bring back thousands of pins to serve as inspiration on this visual discovery engine.

- www.pinterest.com

Supplies

Amazon

Amazon is a fantastic place to find craft supplies on a budget. Offering items from around the world, it's easy to find nearly any craft supply needed through Amazon. Here are a few dedicated areas of Amazon where you can browse through craft supplies:

- **Crafting:** www.amazon.com/crafting/b?ie=UTF8&node=378733011 or https://amzn.to/2RYEZES

- **Craft supplies:** www.amazon.com/craft-supplies/b?ie=UTF8&node =8090710011 or https://amzn.to/2Stjlo9
- **Arts, Crafts, and Sewing:** www.amazon.com/s/ref=lp_378733011 _ex_n_1?rh=n%3A2617941011&bbn=2617941011&ie=UTF8&qid =1549995616 or https://amzn.to/2GmkUXH

Etsy Craft Supplies and Tools
Once again, this immense website dedicated to offering handmade items from crafters around the world is a fantastic resource for craft supplies. A simple search of the website will likely provide you with whatever supplies or tools you need, but here's a link to the craft supplies and tools section of Etsy, perfect for browsing:
- www.etsy.com/c/craft-supplies-and-tools

Craft Stores
There are many brick-and-mortar stores as well as online stores that stock craft supplies in particular. Here are just a few of them that you may check for your supplies:
- **Michaels:** www.michaels.com
- **AC Moore:** https://acmoore.com
- **Dollar Stores:** www.dollarstore.com
- **Dick Blick:** www.dickblick.com
- **Joann Fabrics and Crafts:** www.joann.com
- **Hobby Lobby:** www.hobbylobby.com

INDEX